Battered, Beaten and Scorned
Still I Rise Above It All

Book 1 of 2

My Rising Years of Hell

Battered, Beaten and Scorned
Still I Rise Above It All

by Sandra Barnes

Book 1 of 2

My Rising Years of Hell

Editor
Ravi Gurumoorthy

Senior Editor
Johnathan Patterson

Senior Publisher
Steven Hill

ASA Publishing Corporation
ASA Publishing Company

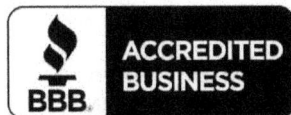

A Publisher Trademark Copy page

ASA Publishing Corporation
An Accredited Publishing House with the BBB
www.asapublishingcorporation.com
Landmark Building
23 E. Front St., Suite 103, Monroe, Michigan 48161

Copyrights©2017 Sandra Barnes, (Realistic Writing Incorporation LLC)
All Rights Reserved
Book Title: Battered, Beaten and Scorned Still I Rise Above It All (Book 1 of 2)
Subtitled: My Rising Years of Hell
Date Published: 03.09.2017 / Edition 1 *Trade Paperback*
Book ID: ASAPCID2380699
ISBN: 978-0692739570
Library of Congress Cataloging-in-Publication Data

This book was published in the United States of America.
State of Michigan

A Publisher Trademark Title page

Acknowledgment

"Thanks to Mr. Stacy, Church Pastors, My Family, Friends and Many others for their support and shoulders to cry on and their listening ears. It's because of you guys *I Rise Above It All!*"

Sandra Barnes

Special Dedication

To my late son,

"Chester Tremaine Mack"

I thank God for allowing me to have a wonderful son whom been in my life for 26 years. He gave me a lot to look forward to. Without him always encouraging me to use my talent to help someone else, I wouldn't have never made it possible.

I thank God for putting Paul in my life so that I can have a story to share about my struggles, love, heartache, and a lesson learned not to allow myself to go through that type of life again with anyone else.

Sandra Barnes

Introduction

I am a 32-year-old single mother raising two children on my own and alone. Living in a rural area in a small town with my mother and three brothers. While living here you only have a poor choice of finding a man to be a good soulmate and a good father. Mostly all the good men are spoken for or in a marriage, and that is not a choice I am planning to make.

Tired of the lonely nights, holidays, birthdays, etc. I begin to pray for someone to come into my life to help me raise my children, and to help guide them in the way that they should go; teach them morals and principals to become a good man and a good woman.

After praying and waiting for that someone, months later Paul then comes into our lives. And not knowing what I was asking for, our lives became a living hell.

Soon after being with Paul for short period of time, here comes with him – are the mind games, and the tiptoeing through the minefields in our very own home. In my mind, I am never allowed to let my guard down. We all become mentally and physically abused by the hands of this man, *Paul*. The man I thought that was the love of my life.

Over the years, I lose the love and respect from one of my children, and the other is so afraid for my life that he just wouldn't allow himself to leave home, and to go on with his own to become the person that he was meant to be. The scars become so deep until the love I have for this man turns into hate, but in my heart, I just couldn't find the way to walk away.

Suffering through the pain and abuse that I endured all because of a promise I made to stay in his life in order to help him become a better person. Over the years he made promises that were always broken, . . . and also my heart.

Praying for so long for all of this to come to an end, until finally one day it all happened through an unnatural incident.

. . . But before that time came, I was *Battered, Beaten and Scorned*.

Table of Contents

Battered, Beaten and Scorned *Still I Rise Above It All*

Book 1 of 2

Acknowledgment
Special Dedication
Introduction
Table of Contents

My Rising Years of Hell

Battered, Beaten and Scorned
Still I Rise Above It All

by Sandra Barnes

Book 1 of 2

My Rising Years of Hell

JUNE

1 9 9 4

Chapter 1

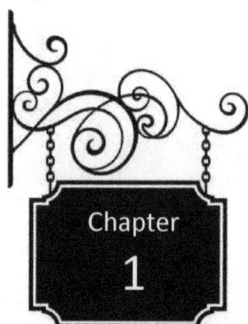

As I am walking home from work, I decided to stop by the store to pick up a few items that I needed. Upon entering into the store, I notice there's a group of men standing around watching me as I pass by. In the crowd, there's one guy staring me down. I begin to get nervous about how he's standing there looking at me. I then go into the store; there I am taking my time hoping that by the time I'm finished with my purchase he would no longer be outside. After purchasing my items, I then leave out of the store, but to my surprise he's still here. As I begin to walk away, I call one of the men I've known for a long time to walk me half of the way to my mother's house. While walking I began to ask questions about the man watching me, he says to me that his name is Paul; never hearing of him I ask no more questions. After getting home I called a friend – I begin telling her about my encounter and the feeling I got from this man while walking pass by the name of Paul. After talking with her for a while about this we decided to call it an evening and then we got off the phone.

Getting myself and my children prepared for the following day, I am trying to figure out how to avoid this man if he's there by the store again when I go tomorrow. Meanwhile, my children are now settled down . . . but for me, it was hard trying to get this guy off my mind. So, I decided to leave and go across the street to my neighbor's house. While socializing with my neighbor, I realized that the time begins to pass so quickly. Being that I have an early start in the morning, I left and went home to settle myself down for the night.

The following day after seeing my children off to school, I leave the house walking to work. While passing the store there's Paul standing against the wall. I then begin to walk faster – hoping that he doesn't follow me. Making it to work and still thinking about this guy, I am also trying to figure out what he is up to. My day is now over due to the fact I am leaving early, regretting that I have to return home the same way I came. As I get closer to the store I am not looking forward to seeing that man. Luckily upon arriving there, he was nowhere in sight except for the man who walked me home yesterday standing in the same spot calling me over to him – telling me that this guy who I'm very leery of wants me to know that he is very interested in me. My thoughts of seeing this guy Paul standing in the crowd looking like a bum wasn't much to second guess, I told him "No thanks." After getting home, I go into my brother's bedroom sit on his bed and says to him I think I am about to have a problem on my hands. He says to me, "You need to be careful if you are not sure of this guy." After speaking with him I left out of his room.

Minutes later the telephone rings. Upon my mother answering she then hands me the phone. As I was answering the phone to my surprise it is the guy . . . Paul. He introduces himself to me and goes on to say, "I got your number from a personal friend and I wish to get to know you better – and also to become your best friend. If it is possible, maybe we become lovers. If you decide, it will be great. And if not, I will return your number to the person I received it from."

Saying to him, "I will think about it because I have two children that I have to raise."

He then says to me, "I have children of my own but I had

to leave them because I was having problems within my marriage. Also, I was on the verge of killing myself . . . I was thinking about jumping off of the Washington State Bridge when a voice came to me and said *Paul go home there is someone there waiting on you*." He continues on to say, "When I saw your face, that same voice came to me and said *She is the one*." He then asks, "Will you please give me a chance?" I told him that I already have a best friend, but give me your number and I will call you back.

After Paul and I hung up, I went back to my brother telling him about the telephone conversation Paul and I had. He says to me to just make the right decision. After that, I turned and walked out of his room. I then went into my bedroom and laid down across my bed thinking to myself if I should give this guy Paul who I've been trying to avoid a chance. Maybe this is the love I have always been longing for. Calling my children into the bedroom and sitting them down, I ask the question, "How would you guys feel if I start to date?" They both saying to me, "Mom go for it!" I then kiss them both and calls it a night.

Chapter 2

Days have now passed, my formal boyfriend and I started having problems within our relationship. *"I can no longer be the man you want me to be!"* Soon after he said these words to me, I decided to let him know what time it was . . . "I can be comfortable with that because I know it wasn't going to last that long," and after that – I hung up on his behind.

While lying in my bed I started thinking about Paul, so I decided to give him a call. As he answers the phone I can hear the excitement in his voice. After a few minutes getting more acquainted, our conversation was starting to get a little heavy, I started explaining to him that at this point we can only be friends. He agrees. After I got off the phone with Paul, I then called my girlfriend to let her know what was up.

"Hey girl, you know the guy I was talking about earlier, Paul?"

"Yeah, what about him?"

Well I decided to give this guy a chance – only to see where we will go in the relationship."

She said to me, "Make sure you make it work, but most of all think about your children and their happiness."

I responded, "I only hope he can be a good father figure in their lives."

Before hanging up the phone, she then invites me to take a walk with her. I told her, "Sure I will be glad to," then we hung up.

Minutes later I arrived at my girlfriend's house, we then go on our walk. While out walking, we happen to run into Paul, "Hey Sandra, I'll be thinking about you."

Walking away with a smile on my face my girlfriend says to me, "Ooh girl, I think you're falling in love."

I then responded, "I'm not exactly sure, but I am kind of falling in love."

While walking on our way back home my girlfriend says to me, "You just have to go with your heart."

Finally arriving home and getting inside I found out that my mother has already put my children in bed. Minutes later the telephone rings. Answering to a strange sounding voice as I ask to whom am I speaking with, Paul says to me, "I just want to hear your voice . . . and also to say goodnight." After saying our goodnights to each other, we then hung up the phone.

The following morning before getting out of bed, I am awakened by a knock at the door. Upon hearing my mother talking, I decide to go and see who she is talking with. Walking into the living room only to see there is no one in here. She said to me that 'Paul left this big red apple for you, but before walking away, he also said to tell you good morning.' After returning back into my bedroom the telephone rings . . . not to my surprise it is Paul.

"Good morning. I hope you enjoy your apple . . . and you can look for this to happen every morning, every afternoon, and every evening."

I ask, "Why are you doing this?"

He said, "Because you are the apple of my eyes."

Now he got me thinking that he is the sweetest man any woman can meet; but not saying it directly to him. So I just told him thank you and then hung up the phone.

One hour later after seeing my children off to school, I then go ahead and get my day started. Upon walking into the kitchen I am being questioned by my mother. "Are you sure Paul is the one you want to spend your life with?" Giving no answer in return, I then go outside to clear my head. At this point I am questioning myself, but I am really tired of being alone. Becoming frustrated from the question that I have been asked, I went back inside and without saying nothing to anyone I go back into my bedroom; lying across my bed and falling sleep. Shortly afterwards, I am awakened by hearing the voices of my children coming into the house. I then get up out of bed and go to greet them home. After getting them prepared for the next following day like I usually do, we all settle ourselves in for the night.

Weeks have gone by with all the passing by of each other and the telephone calls, I finally get the chance to sit and talk with him face to face. It was 3:00pm as my children and I are sitting here in the backyard underneath the tree when Paul walks up. While walking over to me and my children I begin introducing him to them, my daughter being the youngest and the friendliest she really seems to like him a lot. My son on the other hand is just standing here staring him in the face. After introducing Paul to my children and getting their reaction, I then take him on the inside to introduce him to my mother and my grandfather. My mother seems to be very fond of him, but my grandfather having nothing to say at all. I Allowed my children to go and spend time with their friends while Paul and I sit down to get to know each other a little better.

"Sandra, if you just give me the chance I really want to be in you and your children lives . . . and I will be the best man I can be."

As he continues to go on and on, I said to him *but in a nice way*, "The only way you can be in our lives is that you have to change your looks and dress better than the way you are now. Also, you have to get a job."

He responded, "If that's what it takes . . . it will be done." Then he kissed me on my cheek and said, "I have to leave now, but I will be seeing more of you."

Upon leaving my mother's house and walking Paul to the side of the road I kissed him on the cheek and we said our goodbyes. Minutes later, my children return home. After settling down, we went into my bedroom to have a little talk. Explaining to them that I made the decision to give Paul a chance to be in our lives – they both are just sitting here not saying a word. Also, explaining to them that I will not be forcing them on Paul; this new man in my life.

The next following day rolled around and I had to stop by the grocery store on my way back from work, so I decide to pay a visit to Paul's Mothers' house in which she lives only just across the street from the store. As I am leaving the store and noticing Paul's mother standing in her doorway, I decide to just walk on over. Upon walking in the yard and as I get closer to the door, she began moving away from the door. When I finally walk onto the porch, she shuts the door. Knocking on the door to my surprise, she only opens it halfway.

After speaking to her I then ask, "May I speak with Paul?"

Saying to me in a mean tone of voice, "No he is not here! He should be here shortly."

As she attempts to slam the door in my face, I stick my foot on the inside and push the door open. She then gives me this look and tries to slam the door again. After sticking my foot in the door for a second time, she said to me – still in a mean tone voice, "You can come in and have a seat!" As soon as I get inside and start to sit down, she began telling me about her son.

"Just to let you know, Paul has a wife and children that lives out of town . . . and there's no telling when he will leave."

Ma'am, I also have children and a husband that lives out of town. And if I decide, I also can leave."

She then goes on to say, Besides, since he has been home

all types of females have been coming by to pay him a visit."

No longer wanting to hear about other females I then decide to leave. Upon walking out her door, I turned around and said to her, "Just let Paul know that I stopped by." In the mist of all this while walking back across the yard, I forgot an item when I was shopping that I really needed, so I then return back to the store. And just as I am picking up the item there's this voice in my ear saying to me "You look good enough to eat." Turning around only to see it is Paul standing here. After saying hello and saying to him I stopped by your mother's house to see you but there was something she said to me that I do not care to hear, Paul said to me that I should pay no attention to his mother because she has very funny ways about herself.

As I am walking out of the store Paul asking, "Can I walk you home?"

I replied, "Are you sure this is what you want to do?" Meanwhile walking home and wanting to know more about the females. While still speaking on the subject, Paul says to me that they are some of the ones I were friends with before he left home, and it should not be a big deal.

Finally getting to my mother's house I invited Paul to come inside . . . he then accepts. As I put away my packages and begin to make supper for my children and myself, Paul requests that he makes a special dish for us. By allowing him to do so, he makes something quick and simple. Three hours later, Paul is now ready to leave. Walking him to the door, I kiss him on the cheek and we said our goodnights.

The following morning I am being awakened by my mother screaming down the hallway. Jumping out of bed to see what is the problem, she hands me the telephone. Answering the phone only to hear the voice of Paul saying to me, sorry for waking you so early, but I will be there in a little while to spend some time with you. Not wanting to get up so early I go ahead and get dressed. One hour later, Paul shows up at the door. To my surprise, he has a neat haircut, his face shaved, and he has on nice clothing. Not looking like the same person, he says to me, I am here to claim the woman I always wanted.

Noticing that my children are dressed, Paul then asks, "Can I please walk your children to the store because I would like to spend a little time with them if it is okay with you?"

Shortly after allowing my children to leave with Paul, my brother comes up to me asking, "Why do you trust your children with that man when you only know so little about him?"

I told him, "If I am going to be in a relationship I have to build trust."

Walking away my brother shaking his head, "You cannot trust everybody."

Being that Paul and my children have been gone for a long period of time and hearing my brother, I have now become nervous.

As I walk out of the house to go and find my children, there was a car pulling into the driveway – it was Paul and my children getting out of the car. Walking pass me as if something is wrong my son just goes on inside without saying a word. Once we all got inside I wanted to know what was up . . . I then questioned Paul, "What went wrong with you and my son?" Paul saying quickly in response to me before I really get upset, he was telling me that taking my son to get a haircut he got mad about him doing so. Now by knowing my son, and finding this very hard to believe. It has gotten late and it is time for him to leave.

After giving him time to make it home, I decided to give Paul a call. Upon calling Paul's mother to make sure he made it home, she said to me that she hasn't seen Paul since he left here earlier today, so if I'm looking for him she hopes that I find him wherever he may be. Giving it no second thought, I hung up and ended my night in wonder . . .

Chapter

3

Days later, I haven't heard a word from Paul. People are now coming to me saying they have been seeing Paul hanging around the crack house because it was happening daily. Being told not to believe everything you hear, I try to ignore what they are saying. Wanting to call and confront Paul on the hearsay, I don't even bother.

Shortly after, I received a call from my ex-boyfriend requesting to stop by and visit my children. I said to him that it will be okay, but he can only stay for a little while. I had no idea that he was only one block away from my home until he told me. I hurried up and informed my mother of my ex-boyfriend stopping by to visit my children; he was still like a best friend to me. After she said to me that it will be okay, he then pulls into the driveway. Watching my children running outside to greet him as he approaches makes me wonder rather or not I am making the right decision.

While sitting here in the living room suddenly there's a knock at the door. My mother went to answer it. When she opened the door, I heard her say, "Where did you come from?" Going to see whom she is talking to – and boy was I surprised to see who was standing there before us, . . . Paul. Coming inside he introduces himself to my ex-boyfriend.

After Paul introduced himself, he then asked the question, "Why are you here?"

My ex-boyfriend replied, "Maybe for the same reason you are here."

Paul kept nitpicking at him until a bad argument broke out between the two. At this point my mother's boyfriend gets up out of his chair – standing in the middle of the floor saying, "This has to stop because this argument has gotten out of control, and there are children in here!"

Out of nowhere Paul said to my ex-boyfriend, "You should leave or something bad is going to happen."

Trying to calm the two of them down they both turn to me and ask, "Which one of us you want into you and your children's lives?"

Disappointed at the two of them and in shock my mouth couldn't move. Getting up out of his chair my ex-boyfriend saying to Paul that he was going to leave but not because of him – it is out of respect. After walking him to the door; angrily saying goodnight, he gets into his car and drives out of the driveway. Passing Paul sitting here I goes into my bedroom with my children. My son says to me, "Now you see?!" My daughter and I just looking him into his face. Before I can ask the meaning of the remark, my mother says to Paul, "You really need to go into her room and the two of you need talk this out." My children then excuse themselves *meaning* they left out of the room.

Apologizing for his actions he goes on to say that he really cares a lot about me. Continuing to talk and the time passing by, it is now close to being morning. Paul getting ready to leave goes into the living room only to hear my mother say that he can stay and get a few hours of sleep. Returning back into my bedroom and lying at the foot of my bed, he kisses me on the back of my leg – we said our goodnights and fell asleep.

Waking up with the sun shining through the window Paul kisses me on my cheek and then leaves. After he left, I then went into the kitchen and said to my mother, "You were very wrong last night for inviting Paul to come inside – knowing my ex-boyfriend was here." My mother responded by telling me that it was only because I have a tough decision to make. Minutes later the telephone rings, it's Paul.

"Hey baby, I am really sorry about last night, but I have some errands to do . . . but I will call you later."

After promising my children that we'd go out to lunch, we get dressed and leave for the restaurant. Returning home from being out for a few hours and requesting we watch movies until we fall asleep, I agree to their request. It has gotten late and by not hearing nothing from Paul, it is really making me wonder where he may be. Also, hoping that the people are wrong about what they have been saying about him.

July 1st my daughter's birthday. Having already planned something special, but I guess I will have her birthday party. Still wondering why Paul hasn't called. Upon preparing for the party and not expecting Paul, guess who shows up? . . . Paul, walking up the driveway as plain as day. As I go out to begin the grill Paul insists that he takes over. Suddenly my ex-boyfriend also arrives, but this time he is not alone. Before getting out of the car. Paul holding the grill knife and fork in his hand walks over to my ex-boyfriend's car putting the knife against his neck saying to him, "You need to leave!" Seeing Paul leaning forward in the window of the car, I rush over to the car to make sure this does not get out of hand, only to notice the handle of a pistol. So I kindly asked my ex-boyfriend to leave before someone gets hurt, he then cranks his car. But before pulling out of the yard, he looked at me dead in my face said, "You don't know nothing about this man and you are taking his side," and drove off. After him leaving, I continued on with the party acting as if nothing just happened.

Going inside to get the cake my mother was very upset. "I don't know what is going on in Paul's mind, but you really need to talk to him . . . to keep himself in control."

It is now becoming late and I have to bring this party to an end. Taking the children inside for cake and ice cream, Paul walks over to me and kisses me on the cheek and then leaves. Finishing out the party, I then prepare my children to settle down for the evening. As my children are settling down the telephone rings. I answered the phone only to hear my ex-boyfriend saying to me that he will not apologize for wanting to hurt Paul, but he will apologize for his action. Saying to him, "The way you acted is really nonsense."

After hanging up the phone my brother requested that I go with him to shoot a few games of pool to calm my mind. Minutes later, we leave the house and go to the club. As we walk into the club someone walks up to us saying that Paul just walked out a few minutes before we got here. Trying not to get upset I smiled and walked away leaving them just standing there. After shooting a few games of pool I am becoming tired. While walking back home my brother says to me that he really does believe that there is something wrong with Paul, but he just can't figure him out. Returning home and getting inside, I am hoping to hear something from Paul before falling asleep, but knowing it is the weekend I probably won't. After staying up for hours waiting for the telephone to ring, I figure I will call it a night.

Chapter
4

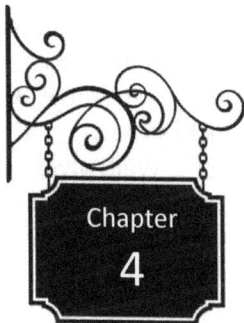

Four days later, the 4th of July, . . . *My Birthday*. Now, my plans were to rest for the whole day, but unfortunately that is not about to happen. My children are now out of bed and my mother seems not to have control of them . . . I think it is on purpose. As I am trying to fall back asleep, there's a knock at the front door. My mother yelling down the hallway saying to me that she needed me to get out of bed and come here. Not wanting to get out of bed but having no other choice, I get up anyway. Upon going into the living room there he is, Paul, standing in the middle of the floor holding a bottle of Champagne and a pint of strawberries. He then hands me the gift and says to me that there's more from where these came from. After taking the strawberries and Champagne into the kitchen and putting them in the refrigerator, I then go and get back into bed.

It's 12:00pm in the afternoon, here he is again with more strawberries and another bottle of Champagne. Again, being woke up out of my sleep I can hear my mother asking Paul, "Are you planning to do this for the rest of the day?"

He said, "Yes, it will happen until I get off from work . . . and that will be 5 o'clock this evening.

Upon hearing the front door being closed *again*, at this point I know it is time for me to get out of bed and get dressed for the day. Not feeling like doing anything, I am just going to be lounging around and playing games with my children. Having the thought that maybe my ex-boyfriend might show up, I then picked up the telephone and gave him a call to see if he has any plans for today, . . . and hoping he does. Well, my ex said yes, which brings a sense of relief to my mind because I am really not up for any arguments. Two hours later, Paul is now showing up at the front door and in his hand he is holding bags with food, balloons, and a small box.

He handed me the box and said, "Open your present now. Opening the box to see it is a gold necklace with a charm . . . on the charm it reads you're special. As he was taking the necklace out and placing it around my neck, my brother says to me, "I guess he sees something special in you." I smiled and then went to look inside the other bags he brought with him and noticed that Paul has all different kinds of meats to be put on the grill. As he goes outside to fire up the grill, my sister and I decide to help prepare the meats. Finishing my part I then go to get into the shower.

Upon showering, the charm falls off the necklace and goes down into the drain. Not being able to retrieve it, now I am thinking to myself how I am going to tell Paul about me losing the charm.

After getting dressed and returning back outside, Paul asked, "Do you like the necklace?"

Saying to him, "Yes." I then go on to tell him that the charm fell off the necklace and went down into the drain.

He responded back to me in a nice manner, but you can hear it in the tone of his voice and about the way he said 'It's okay,' that you can almost feel that it wasn't. He then turns around and asks, "How did it happened when it was on the necklace?" Looking at the expression he has on his face I can tell he is upset. I then return back inside of the house to try once again to retrieve the charm. Being inside for only a short period of time, there is now yelling coming from the outside. Here I come running out the door, only to see that all of my brothers are now upset.

I asked, "What happened?"

One of my brothers says to me, "Your man made a comment that he will take one of us and beat the other two . . . so we insisted that he try and do so!"

Realizing that Paul cannot take on all of my brothers, I try to smooth things over because they will actually hurt this man.

It's about 6:00pm in the evening, people are now beginning to come. Everyone is really having fun and enjoying themselves. For whatever reason my nephew goes into the house, gets my balloons, and then brings them outside and just let them fly up in the air is beyond me. But it's causing me to get upset and I want Paul to do something about it. Instead, Paul says to me that he told him that he can go inside and play with the balloons, but I had no idea my nephew had another agenda for the balloons on his mind, let alone Paul telling him to do so without my knowledge or permission. While discussing the matter with Paul, my sister then gets upset. As the two of us begin to argue, Paul gets his things and leaves. As I'm thinking that he will be returning, I continue on with the cookout.

The sun has set, it's 8:00pm in the late of night, we have a few stragglers, and still no sign of Paul. Nope, he has not returned. And the people are beginning to leave the cookout. After cleaning up the yard and thinking where Paul may have gone, I needed to take a walk to clear my head, so then I decided leave also. Getting tired from a long day and the walking, I decide to go back home. Returning home and going into my bedroom my son comes to me saying, "Mom what sense did that made?" Wondering what he is talking about, going on to say, "Mom, you know Paul started all of the confusing just to leave." Trying not to let him see me upset and to get his mind off of Paul, I then begin joking around with him.

Well, here we are . . . at 10:00pm, and it's now bedtime for me and my children. Explaining to them what happened today that it was all a misunderstanding, and do not take it to heart – we all were a little upset. Laying here, they both just look me in my face and says *Goodnight*.

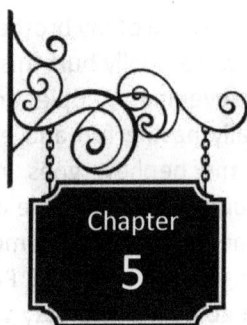

Chapter
5

The following day, here it is 7:00am in the morning and the telephone is ringing. My mother answers it and begin having a conversation with someone while walking down the hallway to my bedroom door. She knocks a few times and says that I need to answer this call. I'm thinking it is someone important because of the reason she says it in the way that she did. To my surprise it is Paul . . . here we go . . .

"Can I have a talk with you?"

"Go ahead and speak."

"Are you doing okay?"

I responded again by saying, "Yes."

He continues with the questions. "Why did you get upset about the balloons?"

"Well, how do you buy someone something and allow someone else to bother it without asking?" I replied.

He then gets smart with me. "Why are you answering me a question with a question?"

I looked straight at the phone and said, "Because I have already explained it to you, and besides . . . it is too early for this!"

He then offers to go and buy more. After saying no to him, he goes on to say to me if it is okay with me, he would like to take me out for dinner. Asking him how was he planning to take me out when neither one of us have a car. After saying to me *'Let me handle this'* he then hangs up the phone. So, upon getting dressed, I decide to do something special for my children on our family day. While taking our nature walk, I start explaining to my children that I am going on a dinner date with this guy Paul and that I am going to be okay, even though I hate to be away from you guys but that I will be returning early. Standing here very silently and not saying a word they both just put down their heads.

Three hours later as I am getting dressed, the telephone rings. Answering only to hear Paul saying to me that he is on his way to pick me up. As I am fixing my children their snack for tonight, Paul pulls into the driveway. Going to the door only to notice that he is driving my sister's car.

"How did you get my sister's car?"

With a surprise look on his face, he said, "We have to go back by and pick her up because I requested that she goes with us."

After picking my sister up from her home, we then leave to go to dinner. While riding down the highway Paul asking, "What is your favorite food?" After saying to him that it was seafood, he then goes on to say, Seafood you shall have!"

Getting to the restaurant Paul gets out of the car, comes around to my side and opens my door. Upon getting out of the car, Paul reaching to hold my hand. Giving him my hand, he then kisses the palm, and we go inside of the restaurant. As we are being seated Paul requesting the finest wine that is being served.

Not wanting to drink because I am not a drinker, I go ahead and have one glass. Upon hearing me placing my order, Paul is saying to me that he wants me to eat as much as possible, to order anything that I see on this menu because he has enough money to pay for it all.

Having such a wonderful moment and glancing at the clock and noticing the time, it is now 10:00pm.

"Oh, . . . look at the time, we gotta be heading home soon."

"Why so early?" asked Paul.

"Because I really need to be at home with my children."

As we are getting ready to leave, he goes and orders two plates to go for my children. Returning from the restaurant, Paul takes my sister home first. Getting out of the car Paul is thanking my sister for allowing him to use her car, and that he really enjoyed her company. As we pull up in my mother's driveway, Paul reaches over takes both of my hands, and then begins kissing each finger one by one. As he gets to the last one, he then reaches over and kisses me on the cheek. Saying our goodnights, Paul says to me that this is not the first, and that he promises me it will not be the last.

While after seeing Paul off, I'm going inside the house only to find my children are not in bed.

"Why are you guys still awake?"

They both saying to me, "Because we were waiting for you to come home, . . . because we figure that man took you away from us."

"Look, . . . that is something the two of you never have to worry about."

While they were sitting at their table I give them their plates. Sitting here we all talk about our day – noticing that they both are getting sleepy. Kissing them goodnight, I then excuse them from the table. We all then call it a night.

Chapter
6

Two days later, it is back to the normal. I haven't heard a word from Paul, nor have I had any visits. Being today is my day to go shopping and not feeling up to the walking, I've decided to go and borrow one of my neighbor's cars. Upon riding to the store, there Paul is . . . walking from the store. Pulling up beside him and asking him in a nice way, "Why haven't you called or stopped by for a visit?"

Standing here with a strange look on his face, he in return says to me, "Why are you asking me questions?"

I said to him, "I have been told that you have been hanging around the crack houses with a lot of different people."

Angrily through the rolled down window, he then begins pushing me up against my head with his hands. As he continues pushing my head around, he keeps asking repeatedly, "Who are they? . . . Who are they?!"

I managed to cut the car off and open the door to get out, but he pushes the door close on me – standing there yelling, "Who are they?!" I quickly climbed across the seat to the passenger side of the car; getting out and walking around to where he is still standing. Now he is saying to me, "If you have to listen to those people that's talking to you, then you leave me the hell alone!"

Saying to him, "I will." Then started walking back around to get into the car. But before I knew it, Paul grabbing me by the arm with force pulling me back to him, asking, "Why are you doing this?!"

"How I am not supposed to believe it when I don't hear from you?"

Paul's justification was "At night my mother takes the telephone into her bedroom and does not allow me to get the phone." Then he fills my mind with another, "The reason for not coming by to visit you, is because I have been getting off from work late."

I looked up at Paul and kissed him on the cheek before getting back in the car, and then turned around and said to him, "I am going to call it quits for now. I need time to think things out – not for myself, but also my children. Driving off I am feeling confused and also thinking to myself, 'Have I just gave up the man that might have been the worst or maybe the best one?' Now returning home from one of the worst moments I have ever experienced in years.

As I am putting away the groceries the telephone rings, not wanting to answer I allow my mother to do so. As I continue to put away my things, she hands me the phone; my mother saying to me it is okay. Still skeptical to answer the phone . . . I did, only to hear the voice of one of my cousins that lives near the night club.

"Hello?"

"Hey cousin. I hate to tell you this, but I saw Paul at this girl's house that lives next door to me, and they were sitting on the porch hugging and kissing on each other."

Continuing to say to myself, 'I knew it was him because he looked me in my face.' But openly saying to her, "Paul and I are no longer talking to each other because I called it quits."

After hanging up the phone, I fix me and my children a light dinner and call it an evening and night.

Chapter

7

It is the month of August, time for children to be returning back to school. Upon waking up this morning and making my children a promise after getting out of school, I will take them shopping. Seeing them off to school, I begin my day by running errands. Wanting to make it home before my children had gotten off of the bus, but unfortunately I am a little late. Pulling into the driveway, they both greeting me at the door saying to me, "Mom you will never guess who is here." Yeah, like I really want to know at this point in time.

Anyway, while walking on inside the house only to see Paul sitting here and having the nerve to ask, "Do you have any plans for this evening?" Trying to ignore him my mother then asks, "What is wrong with you? . . . Paul is talking to you."

I looked at my mom . . . then I turned around and looked at him and said, "I am taking my children shopping."

Suddenly he gets up out of his chair and follows my mother into the kitchen. Hearing her saying *'Thank you baby,'* I begin to wonder what is going on between the two of them. He returns back into the living room and said to me, "I am going with you." Upon saying no, my mother kept begging me to go with him and saying that she will take care of the children while we're out.

As I was getting into the car he asked me, "Where are

you planning to go?" I told him that we (the children and I only, . . . so I thought) were going to the mall. Upon getting to the mall and walking around picking out my children's clothing, Paul decided to volunteer to pick out clothing for my daughter . . . I allow him to do so. Getting to the checkout and taking out my purse, Paul then pulling out his wallet pays the cashier.

On our way home I was thinking about what he did, so I had to ask. "Why did you pay for my children's clothing?"

"Because I am in love with you and I care for your children."

Getting home and going inside, the children noticed that I was carrying the bags which made them become very upset, saying to me, "That is not fair! You went without us even after you made us a promise!"

Paul saying to me, "I am taking them into the kitchen to have a talk."

Seconds later as I am passing by to go into the bedroom they both are rolling their eyes, and at the same time Paul now ready to leave to go home, so we both say our goodbyes and he left. I then went into their bedroom and asked my children, "What did Paul say to the two of you?" They both looked at me and then told me to leave them alone. Pretending to be walking away from the door leading out from their bedroom, they both yell out to me saying, "We don't like him anymore!" After settling myself down I decide to give Paul a call only to see what was said to my children. Upon calling, the phone continues to ring – getting upset, I then hang up and call it a night.

One week later, I haven't seen Paul since the night we went shopping. The morning seems to be going by very quickly as I prepare my children for school and myself for work. Thinking since I have to pass Paul's mothers' house to get to my job, I will go by and pay him a quick visit. After getting to his house and knocking on the door; hoping he will be the one opens it up, but to my surprise it is his mother saying to me, "If you are looking for Paul he is not here, and I do not know what time he will be returning," she then slams the door.

Going on to work and making this count, I don't give the situation with Paul's mother and me a second thought. I could not believe that as soon as I got off from work and got in the house, only to hear my mother say to me, "While you were at work, Paul stopped by and helped your children with their homework and ironed all of your clothes for the rest of the week."

After giving Paul a call and thanking him for what he had done, my son coming to me saying, "Mom, I am about to tell you about the encounter I had with that man," saying to me, "While we were at the barbershop, I was sitting in the chair and he just kept yelling at me when I wasn't doing nothing." He continued, "Also, after leaving out of the barbershop he said to me, 'Make this your last time because I will not be doing this anymore.' He just kept going on and on, so I said to him I don't care because you are not father." Being upset after speaking with my son, I then give Paul a call.

As the telephone continues to ring, finally he answers. Upon speaking, I again ask the question, "What did you do to my son the day you took him to get a haircut?"

He goes on with another different lie saying to me, "We went to the store and your son wanted me to buy him something . . . and by me saying no to him, he got upset."

Knowing he is not telling the truth, I ended the conversation. Then I went over to my children promising the both of them that I will never allow them to go anyplace else with that man alone. Tired from work and needing the rest, I make me and my children an early dinner and call it an evening.

Chapter 8

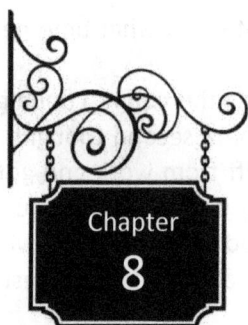

Three months later, it is now Thanksgiving Day. After having to stay overnight with my sister to prepare the dinner and getting up early to go home to get dressed, I then walk out of the door. Upon walking out of my sister's house, there he is *Paul* sitting on his mother's porch waiting. As I am walking out of my sister's yard, Paul gets up off of the porch and walks over to me, says good morning and kisses me on my cheek. As he reaches out for my hand he says to me, "I am not going to be able to spend any time with you because I am going out of town to one of my family members' home, but I will call you when I return." For me the day is going very well. Even though it is not that serious between Paul and me, but I am wishing that we could have spent this day together, but I have to put these thoughts in the back of my mind.

After having dinner and deciding to take my children to the store for ice cream, some female came out of nowhere and walked up to me asking, "Are you and Paul in a relationship?"

I know she didn't just come out her face and asked this, especially in front of my kids. So I said, "No," although I felt like if it was none of anyone's business anyway.

"Why are you asking me that question?"

"I was in your area the other night to see a friend, and on

my way home I saw Paul walking with someone. So I brightened the headlights on my car only to see if it was you that was with him, but shockingly as it may seem, he was holding hands with another female other than you."

You can tell that I was fuming . . . my mixed emotions was on high alert as I was trying to play it off on what Paul said, but instead I told her, "I cannot get angry about a man that is only my friend."

She goes on to say, "Oh, . . . I hope you don't say a word to him about what I just told you?"

I replied, "It is not that important to start an argument because he may not tell me the truth anyway." I then smiled, did an about-face with my children and returned home. When we got in, my children and I took a short nap. As we are napping there's a knock at the door. My mixed emotions was still on high alert . . . I jump out of bed and ran to the door as quickly as I could, only to find out that it is my mother's boyfriend. It is now 10 o'clock at night and Paul have not visited or called me. I am now wondering whether or not if he's at home . . . I pick up the telephone and give him a call, but no one answers. Having a headache from all the stresses of the day I call it a night.

Three days later – Today is Sunday. After returning home from church my children and I sit down to have dinner together. As we are eating they both ask me the question, "Is that man coming over to see you this afternoon?" Then I said to them that we are not going to worry about that man, this is our day. They then said in return to me that this is *your* day because we would like to go and play. Allowing them to go and play with their friends I begin a little house cleaning. Upon cleaning my bedroom there's a knock at the door. Continuing with my cleaning, my mother yells – calling for me to come to the front door. Getting to the door only to see Paul standing here, saying to me "Drop everything you are doing because it is a beautiful day, and I will like for the two of us to go for a little walk."

Stopping with what I am doing, the two of us then leaves to go for a little walk. While walking, Paul reaches for my hand to caress it into his; we then stopped walking. As we stopped, he gazes up at the sky and begins imagining figures that is being made by the clouds. I'm trying so hard to enjoy the moment, but in the back of my mind I'm a train wreck. I am wanting so badly to ask him where has he been for these last two days, but I am going to let him enjoy the moment as well.

Walking for almost an hour and getting a little tired I am now ready to return home. When we finally got home to my place, I invited Paul to stay a while. We both then went inside so I can make my usual rounds on preparing my children for the following the day. It is now eight o'clock pm, Paul and I go outside and sits on the front porch to watch the stars. While sitting here watching the stars, Paul begins pointing out his favorite ones.

While he was still staring up at the skies, I said to him, "This is not something I like to do, only because of a past experience I once had.

Paul snapped out of his twilight and said, "Don't kill the romance." But by the look on his face I can tell he is now ready to leave . . . to go wherever he needed to go. After telling him I have to go back inside to make sure my children stay in bed to get their rest for the following day, I kissed him on the cheek and told him goodnight.

Chapter
9

It is the *Month of December* – This rollercoaster of not seeing much of Paul is really getting the best of me, so I have decided to start spending more time with my best friend and her husband. Being invited over for dinner this afternoon, I go ahead and get my children's things prepared for the following day. Wanting to . . . but not wanting to call Paul, it's time to focus on me, so I continue on with my day.

Hours have now passed, and it is time to join my friends for dinner. Arriving to my girlfriend's home and only being here for a short period of time there's a knock at the front door. When she opened the door, my girlfriend turned to me and said, "Hey hun, there is someone out here who wishes to speak with you." Thinking that it may be Paul, but to my surprise it is my ex-boyfriend. Walking outside of the house and towards my ex-boyfriend, he invited me to get in the car and said that he would like for me to take a little ride with him, that it will only be for a moment. Upon pulling out of the driveway, he then put in one of his favorite tapes. At this point, it is quiet between the two of us. Riding along he turns off on to this dirt road and stops the car. After coming to a halt, he gets out walks around onto my side opens my door requesting that I step out.

While helping me out of the car he said, "You really broke

my heart."

I asked him, "How did I break your heart?" However, before he can answer I then asked, "Why are we out here in the middle of nowhere?" Without giving me an answer, he slaps me in my face. I am standing here in shock because he never attempted nor hit me before.

Taking a minute to realize he hit me, I punched him in his face. As he tried to hit me again I begin to walk away. As he was catching up with me he immediately grabs me by the arm. Seeing a stick lying on the ground near my feet I reach down and picked it up. Without pause of reaction I then swung the stick and hit him on his right leg with all of my strength and said, "Take me home or I will walk!" Holding my face I get back into the car, while he slides behind the steering wheel holding his leg.

On the way taking me home, neither he nor I are saying a word to each other. As he pulls into my driveway I jump out and runs inside of my house leaving him still sitting in his car. Hearing him pull out of the driveway, I go into the bathroom to look in the mirror at my face only to notice my lip is busted. Coming out of the bathroom, I am trying so hard not to let my mother and my brothers notice this abusive injury; my lip was swollen and bleeding – I hurried into my bedroom. One hour later, as I am lying here in my bed the telephone begins to ring – not bothering to get up. My mother bringing the phone to the front door of my room saying to me that I need to answer this. I opened the door midway and grab the phone to answer it only to hear my ex-boyfriend say to me, "I am really sorry, but you don't understand . . . I love you . . . and I didn't intend to hurt you in any way."

With tears falling from my eyes I shouted through the mouthpiece of the phone, "You already have – and I no longer want to talk about it . . . nor do I want to talk to you anymore!" I then hung up the phone.

The following morning, I am really not up to answering no questions about my lip if anyone should ask what happened.

Shortly after getting me and my children dressed for the day, Paul arrives at the door. Hearing my mother inviting him to come in, I hurried up and searched for a piece of rag or something to put around my mouth – I finally found one to cover it up with. Upon hearing him coming down the hallway, I jump into my bed and turned my back so he cannot see the rag that's covering the injury around my mouth. As he comes into my room he sits in my night chair that's next to my bed. He then says to me, "I am very sorry for the way I have been acting toward you." Not wanting him to see what happened to my lip, I am lying here pretending to be asleep. Suddenly, he gets up out of the chair comes lean forward and kisses me on my cheek, asking, "Did you hear what I said to you?"

Not thinking as I am saying to him *it's okay* the rag falls from my mouth.

"What happened to you?"

Not wanting to lie to him, I explain to him the whole story of what happened – saying to him, "I had a fight last night but it is nothing to worry about."

Paul then walks out of my bedroom and goes into the living room with my mother and my brothers asking them, "Did any of you guys see her face?"

My mother then calls me out of my bedroom. As I walk into the living room, she asks, "Why am I the last to know about what happened to you?"

I then responded, "Because this is my problem to handle." Paul being upset insists that the two of us go for a walk. "Paul, I am really not up for a walk right now," I told him.

After continuing to insist that I go walking with him we then leave. While on our walk he continues to ask me, "Is it now over with you and your ex-boyfriend?"

Trying to get him to understand that it was over before I met him – it is as if he's not trying to hear anything I have to say, and continuing to go on and on about nothing. I said to him,

"Since you don't want to hear nothing I have to say, I am going back home."

As I am headed back towards home, he is just standing there in the middle of the road looking at me. Seeing that I am serious, he begins to walk. Paul then catching up with me, grabs me by the arm, and said, "I just don't like what happened."

Upon us both walking into the yard, it is just my luck my ex-boyfriend pulls into the driveway. After getting out of his car he says to me, "I am only here to speak with your children . . . not to cause any trouble."

I said to him, "You really need to leave, because this is not a good time for you to be here."

Paul then begins walking over to him insisting that he hits him in the face. They both then begin to argue; cursing back and forth at each other. My mother standing in the front doorway with a broom in her hand – yelling to my ex-boyfriend to leave out of her yard before she comes outside. After getting back into his car and leaving, Paul begins yelling at me.

"Why would you not let me hit him the way he hit you?!"

"What would you have accomplished hitting him in the mouth?" I questioned.

"I would have accomplished a lot!" He then starts walking further away from the house; still yelling, "You know what? . . . It's over!"

As he continues to leave also, with his back now facing me, I then yell back, "How many more times do I have to hear that coming from you?!"

Not to think about Paul and my ex-boyfriend, I decided to go and shoot me a few games of pool. So I called my children into the living room and explained to them that I have to go and clear my mind. They both saying to me that they didn't want me to go, but I told them that this is a must. My mother then approaches my children and told them that they have to give her this time to herself, and that she will be okay. They both then went into the bedroom.

As I walk into the pool room and begin shooting a game of pool, there's this female that Paul hangs around with walking up to me and insisting that I go with her for a ride. I asked her why and she said that it was because she was a little high and that she needed me to drive. Getting into the car I am wondering where are we going. As we're riding down the highway, all of a sudden she says to me to turn here – at these old run down apartments. Once we parked, she gets out of the car and tells me to stay put while she goes inside one of the apartments that is directly in front of us, and that it'll only be for a minute. When she got inside she then draws the curtains open . . . there Paul sitting around a table with other people. 'Oh, heck no!' . . . After seeing him sitting there, I then honk the horn for her to come outside. As she gets back into the car she says to me that everyone that I have seen sitting around that table is getting high. I told her that if I would have known she was going to take me there like that, I would have stayed at the pool room and continue to play my game.

Returning to the pool room, I get out of the car and begin to walk back home. Arriving home only to find my children are already in bed and my mother is still awake. Upon going into my room to settle down the telephone rings – hearing my mother saying, "I really don't think she needs to talk to anyone." I then walk out of my bedroom and answered the phone only to hear Paul say to me, "I am just waking up after leaving your home earlier . . . I came down with a headache and I needed a nap." By Paul not knowing that I have just seen him sitting in the crack house, I decided to go right along with it – not wanting to hear anymore lies, so I told him that I was tired and I will call him tomorrow. I then hung up the phone.

Chapter
10

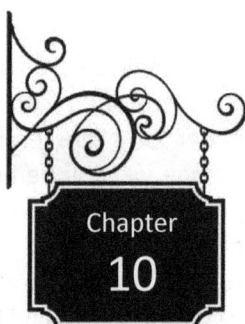

It is now a few days left to go before Christmas. After returning home from work, I was just about to unwind for the rest of the evening when all of a sudden my mother walks up to me saying that she have some bad news to tell me. I decided to sit down in order to hear what she had to say. She told me that my girlfriend's husband has been shot and that I need to go over there. Shockingly, I managed to pull myself together and was able to leave.

Once I arrived at her home she invited me inside and said to me, "I know it has been many years since you saw your husband, but you really need to take your son to see his father – only because my children will never see their father again."

Thinking about what she has just said to me, I responded, "I will be the one to make that decision, only because my son hasn't seen his father since he was one year of age."

Being with her for a few hours it is now time for me to return home, so we said our goodnights and then I left. Once I returned home and got inside I grabbed the telephone and took it with me into my bedroom so I can have some privacy to give Paul a call. Once he got on the phone I told him that my son and I will be leaving out of town for a little while and it will be on Christmas Eve, and that we are going to the State of Mississippi to visit his father.

Paul getting all upset asked, "Are you planning to return?"

I replied, "Yes, because I am leaving my daughter here."

For some reason or another I should have known this was going to happen, now I'm on the phone talking for hours with this man trying to convince me to change my mind – telling me that he may not be here when I return home. Well, after he calmed down a bit, we then said sour goodbyes and I hang up the phone. But, as soon after I started getting prepared to settle down for the night the phone rings, this time it's Paul calling me. "Why have you waited until I have fallen in love with you, . . . and you want to leave?" To me, my son was my priority, so I told him that I made a promise to my son that I cannot and will not break. And that was the end of that conversation.

Christmas Eve has finally arrived. As I get up early to prepare me and my son for our trip, the telephone rings – and not to my surprise, it is Paul.

"What time are your guys leaving for the bus station?"

"Our bus departs at 10am and I will be leaving home . . ."

Shortly before saying another word, he hangs up the phone. Soon as my son and I are walking out of the door, Paul pulls up into the driveway. He then gets out of his mother's car, walks over to me, kisses me on my cheek, and returns back into the car and drives off.

One hour later, my son and I are now sitting here at the bus station. Once we got into our seats on the bus; having eighteen hours before making it to Mississippi, we get comfortable for the ride there. The trip went pretty fast, and now we are here in Mississippi. After arriving into the station and getting off the bus, we were very disappointed because my husband was supposed to be here waiting for our arrival, but he's not. After making several phone calls he finally shows up.

Upon leaving the bus station and thinking that since we're all together we're going to be staying at his place, he takes us to a motel instead. He hands me a room key and then tells the both of us that he is having some work done to his home, but he will be here with us for the stay – and then he turns around and leaves.

Hours have now passed, it's *Christmas Day*, and my husband has not returned. Thinking that my husband was bringing him Christmas gifts, but feeling more like we were abandoned at a hotel, my son is now very upset, saying to me, "Mom I'm ready to go home. I have seen my father and I really don't like him. He acts as if he's not my father." It hurts me deeply to my heart to hear him say that about his father.

Not having the chance to unpack our clothing, I then decided to call the bus station and made arrangements to return home the following morning.

That following morning we were on our way back home. As we are getting closer to home, when the bus finally stopped to take a break – giving the passengers time to stretch their legs, I was looking for a telephone to give Paul a call . . . only to make sure he is still in town. When he answered the phone I can hear the excitement within his voice, "I am so excited to hear from you! Look, I will be at your mother's place when your return."

Hours later, we are now back at home.

As we were getting out of the car Paul greets me with a dozen roses and a card saying to me, "I have to leave but I will be in touch with you later."

Getting inside to unpack and making myself comfortable, I ended up falling asleep. Not knowing how long I have been asleep, my mother awakens me by yelling into my room through the door saying, "Get up! I have supper ready for you!" Even though that I still didn't feel very hungry at the time, I still got up and went into the kitchen. When I saw my mother I asked her if Paul had called or stopped by, but she told me no and not to worry myself about him either; she then walks out of the kitchen.

Being so tired from the ride and seeing that my mother had already fixed me something to eat, I went ahead and finished my supper, then went straight back up into my bedroom and called it a night.

YEAR

1 9 9 5

Chapter
11

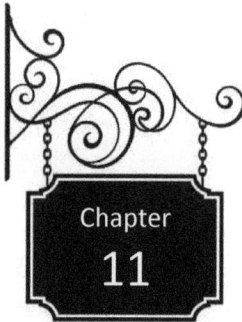

It has now been years that went by and things has gotten very serious. Paul has started coming by the house everyday with a different gift. On his paydays, he is giving me half of his pay check. I am beginning to think maybe people are trying to make him out to be someone he is not.

Meanwhile, Paul calls, "Are you available for tonight?"

As much as I hated to tell him but my answer is yes. And immediately after the reply he wanted to know if I'm already dressed. So I told him that I was, then he said that he will be seeing me in about 10 minutes.

While standing on the porch Paul and another couple pulls into the driveway. He gets out of the car telling me that he is taking me out. We both get back into the car, and I started to wonder where is he is going to be taking me.

"Hey Paul, . . . by-the-way, where are we going?"

"Ah, don't worry . . . I'm going to show you a good time while we are out!" An hour later, we arrive at this fancy restaurant.

After getting out of the car we all went inside together. Once we got in and the doors began to close, I found myself noticing how the whole atmosphere is very romantic. Looking at each other and enjoying our dinner, Paul gazed into my eyes,

"We're not going back home tonight."

"Why not?" I asked.

With this subtle grin on his face, "We're staying at a hotel."

"Paul, I know you're trying and everything, but I do not like staying away from my children too long."

"Babe, calm down . . . I have paid your mother to take care of them."

Upon arriving to the hotel, Paul gets out of the car comes around and opens my door. While standing outside of the car, I begin having thoughts of my children. As he goes inside of the hotel to obtain the key to the room for the night, I then decided to look for a telephone. Trying to call and check on my children I seem to not be having any luck. Since this being my first time being alone with him for a long period of time I am becoming very nervous.

While here sitting on the bed, Paul comes and sits next to me saying in a soft tone, "Relax, . . . relax, I am not going to hurt you." He then begins pulling off my shoes and then my clothing. Laying here nervous and naked, in return he does the same.

As we get under the covers and start making love to each other, I begin asking myself that one magic question, *'Is he the one for me?'* The following morning we returned home.

After getting out of the car Paul informs me that he will be working late this evening, and that he will call me when he gets home.

Time has been passing by very fast, yet still I have not seen nor received a call from Paul, wondering rather or not everything is okay. Not wanting to, but I decide to give him a call. Upon giving him a call, I was hoping he will answer but to my surprise his mother answered instead letting me know that she hasn't seen Paul since the night before. After speaking with her I then hung up.

Trying to keep my mind together, I then went outside to take a short walk. As I am walking, I run into this man that is always hanging around the store that I usually pass by on my way to work.

As we are walking he asks, "Are you looking for Paul?"

Just to keep him out of my personal relationship with Paul, I said, "No, I am not."

He then goes on to tell me anyway, "If you are, he is standing around the corner."

Wanting to know what he is trying to say, I decided to allow my adrenaline to run with this, "Why are you telling me this? . . . What is it for you to gain?"

"Look at it this way boo, I am not looking to gain anything, I just don't want to see you get hurt."

Soon after he said that, I then walked away without saying a word. Feeling determined to go around the corner to see what is going on, I changed my mind and decided to just go home.

After getting in the door of my house, I went into my bedroom and laid across my bed. My children can tell that something was wrong, so they followed behind me and came in as well.

"Mommy, what's wrong with you?"

"Nothing for the two of you to worry about." I then get up and get them settled in before we call it a night.

Chapter
12

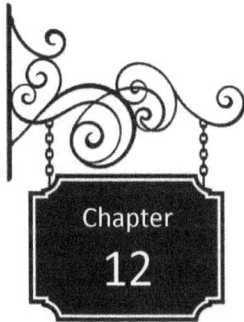

The next day, I received a phone call from Paul. "Did you call me last night?"

"Yes, . . . I did," knowing that this whole conversation was going to be another lie forthcoming . . . but let's hear it anyway.

"I was in my room reading a book and I fell asleep, and my mother never told me that I had a phone call."

I immediately pulled the phone away from my ear, looked at it with this crazy look on my face – as if I just got a call from a telemarketer. Then gaining all sensibility, put it back up to my ear and told him, "You know what? . . . I know your mother doesn't like me, but why would she have told me you were not at home?"

"Ah, don't worry about her because I have something very important to talk with you about. I will tell you when I get to your house."

We then hung up the telephone.

It was about 12pm when Paul arrived. When he came to the door he requested that the two of us should go out into the backyard to talk for a few minutes. After we reached the back he started talking about him looking at a house and that he will be moving in a few days, and that if me and my children would like to move in with him, we are welcome to come. But, if not, this was okay too except that he would much rather have us together.

I paused for a few moments to get my thoughts together while he stood there patiently waiting for an answer. Then I informed him that I would have to discuss this with my mother and my children. Once we got back inside the house and before I can say a word, Paul begins discussing it with my mother and my grandfather. My grandfather not having a problem with me moving out, but my mother on the other hand becomes very upset. She looked straight into his face and said, "She can move out, but the children . . . oh no . . ., will not be going with the two of you."

I turned around and told her, "Mama, I am not leaving my children here."

She continued, "How are you going to get around when you don't have any transportation?"

Paul looked at me, then looked at my mother and said, "There's nothing for you to worry about."

My children on the other hand really don't want to move. I had to reassure them that everything will be okay and that if we do this, they both will have their own separate rooms. When they heard about this, they then became very excited about the move.

Just getting in the doors from work I hear the telephone ringing, so I answered it. "Hello, this is Paul. "The landlord is on her way to your mother's house so that we can both sign the lease agreement." Minutes later the landlord arrives. After inviting her in we all sat down and went over the agreement together, then Paul and I sign it. When we were done, my mother approached me, "Are you really sure you want to move out?"

"Yes," I said. "I am going to a least give it a try."

Paul then receives the keys.

After having a talk with Paul the other day, I have already packed some of our things within that following night. I have made my decision and I am now ready to move. Therefore, the only thing that was left at this present in time was to sign the papers in which we both did. So, as the landlord was leaving the house Paul let me know that he is on his way out the door as well because he has to go get one of his cousin's trucks so we can begin moving our things into our new home.

One hour later, Paul returns with a truck so we can begin loading everything that we are carrying with us. While packing everything on the truck, I decided to leave my children at my mother's house for the night until we are finished, because Paul and I have planned to set their rooms up as we go along. Upon our way leaving my mother's house I stop at the store to buy something special to make for the two of us. Being this is our first night moving into our place I wanted to make this a romantic night.

After getting all of our things unloaded and placing everything where it needs to go, Paul says to me that he is going to return the truck and that he'll return as soon as possible.

Sitting here waiting for Paul to return it is now beginning to storm. Thinking Paul is on his way back home I go ahead and make our dinner. While making the dinner, I went ahead and ran the water so he can have a nice hot bath. Waiting and waiting, but Paul seems not to be returning. Thinking maybe he is held up in the storm and will be coming home soon. Hours have now gone pass and Paul still haven't returned. Being afraid and upset I then put the food away and went back into the bathroom to let the water out of the bathtub. Not wanting to be here alone, I then go next door to call someone to come and pick me up.

While on my way to my mother's house and worrying about Paul in the storm, I decided to go an extra few blocks to see if I can find him. Riding back and forth to other people's home only to see if he is there. Now I ended up constantly going back and forth from our home, just hoping he will soon show up. After making a few more trips around, I still couldn't find him. I finally gave up and returned home to my mother's house to be with my children for the rest of the night instead of continually searching for this man.

6:00am in the morning rolled around and I decided to go back home again to my house and check. When I opened the door, there he is lying on the couch.

"Where were you last night?"

"The weather was bad and I couldn't make it back."

"But upon my returning, I noticed that you weren't here, so I left."

Paul not knowing that I returned to the house a little earlier – at 5:45am, he didn't know that I already knew he wasn't there. Looking him in his face saying to him, "The weather was not that bad that you couldn't make it home. I have been riding around half of the night and morning looking for you." Paul still trying to explain lie after lie. And the biggest one of them all as he is now looking me directly in my face, he had the nerve to ask me "Did you not see my foot prints in the yard?"

This is really something, he's now trying so hard to get me to go outside and look at the foot prints. I couldn't believe it, so I turned away and headed into the bedroom and began packing my things, Paul coming into the room moments right behind me pleading for me to not leave him here alone.

He said, "Without you here with me I cannot make it, I really need you in my life."

Letting my feelings get the best of me I begin to cry as I unpack my things, saying to me that we are going to be a family now, and that I should go and get my children.

Upon leaving to go pick up my children from my mother's, Paul tells me that he really hopes I'm planning to return. When I got there, my mother told me that she will be keeping the children here until we get settled. I told my mom that I am not going to put my children on her, then I gathered their things and we left. Returning home I noticed that Paul has already made dinner and set up children's rooms. After we all ate, we decided to all call it a night.

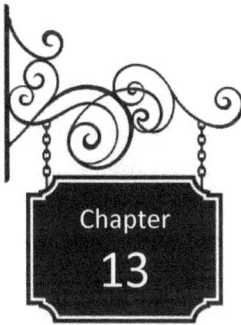

Chapter
13

Weeks have passed, and now the fights and arguments have begun. I have returned back to my old job and was able to make it home earlier before my children and Paul. After being home for a while from work I then began cooking dinner, and also preparing my children's things for the following day of school.

It is now beginning to rain, and to lighten everyone's mood my children and I began watching movies until Paul get home.

6:00pm Paul is being let out of a car in the driveway. I then go to door to greet him home, but when I approached him he kind of pushes me aside and takes a seat on the couch. My children then leaves out of the room, I then go over to Paul and gave him a kiss as I sit on his lap to lighten him up. Playing with him, I firmly push him side the head. Paul said to me that if I do that again he's going to drag me through the mud. Thinking that he is only playing I do it again. All of a sudden, Paul throws me to the floor, grabs my feet and begin dragging me out of the house. Holding up my head to keep from hitting the steps, I begin screaming for help – hoping that the neighbors will come make him stop.

Crying and begging him to stop and to let me go he then drops my feet. As I am lying here on the ground all wet, sore, and cannot move, I took myself a few minutes to mentally readjust, I then get up and run inside before being seen by anyone. As I run straight to the bedroom I took a look at myself in the mirror, I could see that I am bleeding all over from the grass burns only to turn around and realize my son standing at the door shaking his head asking "Why mom?" I don't even have an answer.

Not wanting to go back into the living room to see Paul's face, I went and laid across the bed. Paul following me into the room decided to sit on the bed beside me – telling me that he is so sorry for what he has done, but if he tells me not to do something I should listen to what he has to say. As he is leaving out of the room, he turns around and asked me if I can please forgive him. Not believing this had happened to me, I just can't say a word.

Paul finally leaves out of the room and goes into the bathroom. Hearing the water running into the bathtub I am thinking that he is about to take a bath. Instead, he came back into the bedroom, took me by my hand and led me into the bathroom. Then he took off my clothes and saying to me that I need to get in while the water is warm. Once I got in, he begins washing my body. After having a nice bath like that, I went straight to bed and fell asleep.

The following day I cannot go to work because my body is still sore. Not being able to notice it the night before, I can now see that I have a lot of bruises on my face and arms.

Being home alone for hours I have the chance to get back into my bed – lying here and asking myself the question, "Why are you still here?" And just the thought of knowing that I have nowhere else to go at this time, hurts. I cannot go back to my mother's house because she has already moved other people into her home. I can't afford my own place because I have two young children that I am taking care of, and I am only working on a part time salary. There are no shelters close where me and my children can live, and just knowing no one else will allow me and my children to live with them until I can find my own place.

I then get out of bed and go take me a shower. After showering I began making dinner. My children are now arriving home from school. Walking into the house my son looked me dead in my face and said, "I don't understand you!" and walked away into his bedroom.

Meanwhile, fixing my children their food Paul walks into the house, not saying a word to anyone he goes into the bedroom. When my children and I finished our dinner, they excused themselves from the table and went to their bedrooms. As I sit quietly alone at the table, Paul then comes into the kitchen fixes his food and goes into the living room to have his dinner. When he finished his food, he came into the kitchen – still not saying a word, put his dishes away and then goes into the bedroom. After getting our nightclothes he then heads into the bathroom. While he is running the water in the bathtub he yells for me to come in. Having a little fear but not letting it show. Upon going into the bathroom, he is just sitting here looking into my eyes. As I get into the bathtub, he walks out of the bathroom.

As I am just lying here relaxing. All of a sudden he returns with candles and bubble bath. After lighting the candles he then gets into the tub with me. After taking a warm hot bath we then go into the bedroom. While sitting on the bed, Paul is pulling me closer to him, saying to me that he never wanted to hurt me again.

"Will you please lay down next to me so that I can hold you in my arm?"

Upon lying down, he had me turn my back to him while he wraps his arms around me and then we call it a night.

Two days later, coming home from school my son comes

to me saying that he got into a fight in his classroom. After Paul hearing what was said invites my son to go outside with him. Thinking that he is only taking him out to have a talk, I then begin helping my daughter with her homework. Hearing Paul raising his voice, I stopped and rushed to the front door – seeing Paul pushing my son around. I Rushed out of the house to see what is going on between the two of them. I then pushed Paul away from my son. Paul told me that this is none of my business.

"Paul, my son is my business!" I then sent my son into the house.

"I was pushing him around to teach him a lesson."

"No matter what someone says to him he doesn't have to fight."

Going back into the house, I then ask my son to explain to me what happened at school.

My son said, "A little boy was picking on me; hitting and calling me names. So I punched him in the face."

I told him, "You do not have to allow anyone to beat on you, but the next time tell someone or have your teacher call your grandmother to the school."

Being upset with Paul I said nothing to him for the rest of the evening.

The next day, returning home from work to find my daughter in her bedroom doing her homework. Upon not seeing my son nowhere inside. I begin questioning her of the whereabouts of her brother. She told me that he in the back yard. When I looked out of the backdoor, he was in the backyard standing in the field. I went outside to see what he is doing but as I got closer to him there is blood pouring out of his nose. It is all over his shirt.

I asked him the question, "Why are you out here?"

"Paul told me to pull up the weeds and do not stop until I am finished."

"It is 100° degrees, too hot for anyone to be outside. Go

inside and clean yourself up, I will handle Paul when he comes home."

Getting into the house, I already saw Paul returning home as well. As soon as he started to come in, I told my children to go into their bedrooms. And instead of coming inside all the way, Paul was walking toward the backyard yelling back – on the inside. Paul requests that my son comes outside, saying to my son that he isn't going back out there. Paul finally coming inside and walking down the hallway, he is now yelling to my son asking "What did I tell you do?"

I told my son, "Stop! You are not going back outside in that heat to pull not one more weed."

Paul looked at me and said, "How do you go behind my back and change my rules?"

I said, "If you want those weeds pulled up you go outside and pull them yourself."

Paul pushing me aside leaves out of the backdoor.

My children then begin to get prepared for the following day. Upon calling them into the living room and requesting that they have a seat – explaining to them that I will not let that man hurt you guys in anyway, they both looking me in my face saying, but you are the one that is getting hurt.

It has now gotten late my children are in their beds. I deciding to stay up and watch some television, here comes Paul knocking on the door. He came into house looking so high, I had enough for one evening, so I got up and went into the bedroom. He followed me in the bedroom and then he grabbed me by my arm. I asked him to release my arm but he holds it a little tighter. Trying to push him away he begins hitting me. Remembering the words my father said to me when I was younger, my dad told me that when fighting someone bigger and stronger than you ask God to give you the strength – being that Paul is stronger. I ask for the strength as we began to fight. I grab him and threw him against the wall and then I put my hands around his neck, "I am

tired of what you are trying to do to me and my children."
Thinking that my children are in their room, they heard the two
of us fighting . . . I then let him go. Paul *being so high* goes into
the bedroom and falls asleep. As for me, I stayed on the couch
for the rest of the night.

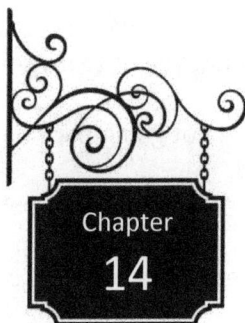

Chapter 14

Two months later, it is very cold outside and the furnace is not
working. Here I am trying to figure out how we are going to stay
warm for today and tonight. Paul has left for work and the
children have left for school, so I decide to go to my mother's
house to stay warm.

Hours later, returning home to find out that Paul have
already went and brought a kerosene heater, leaving a note that
read '*I will buy some oil when I get off from work*.' Upon my
children coming home from school and coming inside they both
begin complaining how cold it is in the house, and that they need
some heat.

Making the decision to make dinner early so the house
can get warm for at least a little while, it was 6:00pm, Paul
returning home grabs a few jugs and informed me that he was to
going to get the oil and will be returning shortly. As usual, Paul

having been gone for so long it is beginning to get annoying, as well as the evening is getting later and colder.

Trying to stay warm my children and I go into our bedrooms to get our blankets so we can have something to wrap ourselves up with, but it isn't working too well for us. We then go into the kitchen and put our blankets on the floor. Turning on the oven and having my children lay down on the floor thinking this will keep them warm but this is not working also. Saying to them to stay inside while I walk next door to make a telephone call because we cannot stay here. After calling just about everyone I knew and having no luck with no one answering their phone. My last result is to call my best friend hoping that he is not upset. Upon answering his phone I explain everything to him about our situation.

He said to me, "You guys go ahead and pack a few things, I am on my way."

After arriving to the house my best friend asks, "Where are you guys going?"

We're going to stay at my mother's for the night."

With an angry look on his face he asks, "Why are you still putting up with this? It is cold and you and your children are being left alone to freeze?"

Cold, upset, and angry, I cannot say a word.

Upon arriving to my mother's house we all get out of the car and started walking up to the door. Getting inside I then call up one of my girlfriends and explained to her what happened. She said to me that she is on her way.

As we're out to go look for Paul to get the oil, we are going to every house I thought he may be at – but I had no luck, I then went back to my mother's house and called it a night.

Early the next morning after seeing my children off to school, I leave to go home. Once I got inside, I went into the living room and saw that the heater is lit and burning. Thinking that Paul is not here, I then go into the bedroom. There he is lying in bed. After hearing me putting my things away he then sits up on the bed and tells me that he couldn't find a ride to come back home last night, so he stayed the night at my mother's because she wouldn't bring him home. Knowing he is not telling the truth, I turned and walked out of the room. As the day goes by, I try not to question myself.

3:30pm my children arriving home from school. All of a sudden Paul gets out of bed and leaves out of the house, both my children saying to me, "Well Mom, he is gone again." I told them that it's not for you guys to worry about. Two hours later Paul returns home with ½ dozen roses and something to make a special dinner with; insisting that I relax until he finishes.

After finishing dinner, Paul calls me and the children to the table. We all then sat around the table talking and enjoying the night.

A few weeks later, upon getting home from work as usual, there was another surprise in stored for me, and this time it was only to see Paul and my children sitting on the porch.

I asked, "Why are you guys out here?"

Paul said, "We're waiting on the police because your children have broken into the house for no reason."

Being upset I said to him, "How are they breaking in if they live here too!"

Paul acting boastfully, "It is my house and they have no right!"

I told him, "If the police come here you are going to be the one that's leaving."

Paul says to me, "Ask your children why they broke into the house."

They both said to me that they have been sitting out here for over an hour and that they got hungry, so they went inside to get themselves something to eat."

Letting them know that it was okay, Paul looked at me directly in my face and said, "You are so wrong!"

Clearing it up, I responded to him that I help pay the bills in this house, and that I also help buy the food. He then takes the beer he is holding in his hand and throws it to the ground, and walks away. After getting inside I say to my children no matter what don't feel bad, you guys done nothing wrong.

After speaking with them and giving my daughter the key to the house, I let her know that after school this is you guy's right way of getting in. The next thing I know it, Paul's coming into the house making fowl comments to my children, saying that you guys have one more time to try and come into the house the way you guys did, and I will have all of you put in jail. After threating my children like that, I had nothing else to say him for the rest of the night.

#####

It is now Thanksgiving Eve, Paul and I first anniversary being together, and also being in our new home, we planned to make our first dinner together. Paul arrives home from work with all the fixings we need for our dinner, including a bottle of champagne and a dozen of roses with a card.

After getting settled down, Paul and I began to start dinner for tomorrow, he then calls my children into the kitchen to join in – my children and I cut and dice the vegetables while Paul makes dinner for tonight, thinking to myself our relationship is getting better. We finish making our Thanksgiving dinner and all the other fixings for tonight.

While sitting at the table eating, Paul decides to invite my mother and his mother over for tomorrow's Thanksgiving feast with us. After dinner, my children went to get ready for bed. Paul and I then spend a little romantic time together and calls it a night.

Thanksgiving Day!

Upon Paul waking me and my children up to a big

breakfast, I am thinking today is going to be a good day. After having breakfast we all get dressed and waited for our mothers to come over for dinner. While waiting, I begin to straighten up with the finishing touches.

As the time passes and no one seems to be showing up, Paul decides to leave us *on this day* at home alone again. So, my children and I have decided to have dinner together anyway.

Being that my son is the man left in the house, I allowed him to carve the turkey. Now that it is beginning to get dark, all of a sudden my sister and mother arrived, but only to spend a little a time with us – and it is only for a few minutes. As they are walking out of the house, Paul shows back up high again saying to me that since his mother did not come to visit us, we're going to go visit her. My sister offering us to ride back with her we all got in the car and left.

Upon arriving to Paul's mothers' house, she asks the question, "Why are you all out so late?" At this point I am asking myself the same question. Paul told his mother that he just wanted to see her. After staying for a short period of time, we return home. I am so disappointed how things have turned out. Paul acting as if he doesn't care about anything, he just goes into the bedroom and slams the door.

As my children and I put the dinner away from earlier today, my son feeling very disappointed said to me, "What a thanksgiving this turned out to be." But I told him that no matter what, we are still blessed. Stopping for a few seconds and thinking on what I said, he then walks away. I took notice of it and then went back to finish my cleaning, soon after that I went into the living room and laid on the couch – calling it a night.

The next morning Paul leaves early for work without saying a word. After my children and I get dressed and leave to go to my mother's house being that I don't have a car, we had to walk five miles. To make the walk safe and easier my children and I walked along the train tracks.

When we finally made it to my mother's house we were so tired to do anything, that I had my children rest for a while before allowing them to go out and play. A few hours later Paul shows up asking how we got here, so I told him plain and simple, that we walked. Of course he got upset, but there was nothing he could do, we were already here. So he left and went back to work.

Now that it is time to go home, I call my children together so we can leave. My sister stopping by to see my mother offers us a ride back to our house. Finally getting home we go inside. I then begin making us a light dinner as my children do their chores. Hours have gone past and Paul hasn't come home yet. My children tired from earlier today decided to go to bed ahead of their normal schedule. I am getting a little worried but knowing Paul, he can only be at two places; either out of town working or at someone else's house getting high. It has now gotten later and I now know he is not coming home, so I secured the house and turned out the lights, then went to bed.

Finally, Paul showing up from the night before . . . I am not asking any questions. Getting inside and looking directly at the disappointment in my face, he couldn't help but come up with the sweetest lie you can ever hear – this time around.

"Look baby, I got off from work late . . . and then, as I got with some friends we started drinking. They ended up leaving, and I couldn't make it home."

So tired of hearing the same ole excuses – just knowing that I can see straight through him, he turns and walks into the bedroom. My children coming into the living room, wanting to sit and talk with me for a bit. While we're sitting here talking about their day, Paul comes out of the bedroom and kneels down beside me saying, "I need your help . . . I have a problem, and I can't do it alone." Not knowing what to say, I looked at him and told him that I was here for him – by his side, but that he would have to help himself. After saying what I felt, he gets up kisses me on my forehead and walks out of the house. My children and I continued on with our talk.

Minutes later Paul and one of my brothers came into the house. Sure enough, yep . . . he is high again. As they are sitting here, someone was knocking at the front door. It is one of the females that hang around next door.

As I open the door she asks, "May I speak with Paul?"

You can imagine my response on what I had to say – and yes, I said it . . .

"You need to leave my house!"

Paul standing behind me looks as if he is lost. But at least when I asked him for his wallet, he did reach into his back pocket and hand it to me, but when I checked he had no money.

So I gave it back to him and said, "Now that you are broke now I am not giving you any of the money back that you gave me earlier today."

My brother standing in the middle of the floor says to me, "It is his money he works for it, and what he does with his money is his business."

Looking at him in shock from what he had just said to me, my response to him is, "I don't care about him working but we live together, and we put our money together to get things done."

Paul getting mad because I made that statement walks out slamming the door. While standing at the door behind him, I told him that if he leaves out of this yard, do not come back. After closing the door and hearing Paul talking to my brother, he told him to go ahead, he rather stay at home. After hearing him say this, I went into the bedroom and locked the door. Afterwards, he did come back inside. Once he secured the house, he fell asleep on the couch.

Chapter

15

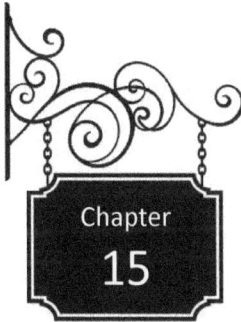

It is one of those days when I just feel like sleeping in, but I know it won't happen. Paul waking up and come knocking on the room door. As he is beating on the door so loud he has now awakened everyone in here. Upon opening the door he comes into the room gets him some change of clothes and goes into the bathroom. He then takes a quick shower. Afterwards, he goes into the kitchen and makes breakfast. He then calls everyone to the table.

While sitting at the table and realizing we don't live far away from the church. I mentioned to my children that we are going to church today. Paul then gets upset and tells me that he just wants to spend the day with me. At this point I can care less what his plan may be, my children and I are getting dressed for church.

After returning home, to my surprise Paul requests that we change out of our church clothing because he has made dinner, and it's already on the table. We then changed our clothing and went into the kitchen. As we sat down, Paul says to us, "When you guys finish, we're going to visit your mother okay?" A little bell is going off in my head *what's the catch* for all of this. Paul goes next door to calls for someone to come pick us up. After being picked up we gets to my mother's house, he tells my children to go visit some of their friends while we sit and talk with her.

While talking, Paul is constantly kissing me – telling everyone how much he really cares for me. I wanted so badly to say something, but I kept it to myself hoping someone will pay attention to the expression I have on my face.

As the sun begins to go down, Paul requests we go for a walk. Not feeling up to it my mother pushes me to go with him. We ended up walking to one of my uncle's houses. There's a lot of people on the inside drinking. Knowing that I have already told him that I wasn't going to spend any money on beer, in front of everyone he decides to ask me to buy him a few cans. I wanted to tell him no, knowing that we are not done paying all the bills. He looks at me and tells me that if I buy the beer, he will replace what I spend. We get the beer and then leave.

While walking back to my mother's Paul is talking and I am not listening because he knows he blew all of his money on last night. We go pickup my children and returned home. Moments later, he's sitting in the living room drinking. The more he pops the tops on the beer, the more upset I become. I think I had enough for one evening. So I get up and went into the bedroom and calls it a night.

A few weeks before Christmas I have gotten another job that requires me to leave the house earlier than before and return home later. Being that my daughter misplaced the house key that I have given her months ago, I made a request to Paul that before the children gets home from school, to come back by the house and open the door so they won't be out in the cold. Lo and behold, I return home to find my children sitting outside. Once we get inside of the house I had my children warm up before preparing for the following day.

Upon Paul returning home I asked, "Were you out of town the reason you didn't stop by the house to unlock the door?" He said that he forgot, but I know he didn't intended to do so.

By not wanting my children to go next door to my neighbor's house because he has different people coming in and out of his home, but at this point I have no choice. As we sit down to dinner, I explain to my children that the things they want for Christmas they may not get them because I am making less money on my new job, and the $500.00 Paul was giving me each week has now gone down to $200.00. They both said to me that they will be happy with whatever they get because they know that man I brought into their lives doesn't want me to buy them anything.

After eating and talking with my children, they got up and went into their bedrooms. When I finished cleaning the kitchen I got in the shower, then off to bed. Paul comes into the bedroom and gets his things and went into the bathroom after hearing the water stopping in the bathtub. I however, rolled over on my side of the bed – not saying a word to Paul when he came back in. He just looked at me for a moment because he knew I was hurting inside, so he left me alone and got in bed and then went to sleep.

It is now a week before Christmas, and after getting home from work me and my children gets settled, soon after we began to decorate the house. I couldn't afford to buy a big tree so we settled for the little rubber one that I purchased upon moving.

While decorating, my daughter decides to put some family pictures together to hang in her bedroom. By having them laying all over the floor and being busy, I forgot to tell her to pick them up before Paul comes home. But before I can say anything to her, Paul walks through the door – coming in and kicking things all around. Not knowing what is his problem, he picks my daughter's pictures off the floor then goes into the kitchen and tears them up and throws them in the trashcan. After telling my children to go their rooms Paul rushes out of the door and gets into the car with someone I've never seen before. I go into the kitchen and get the pictures out of the trashcan, but there's nothing I can do with them to make my daughter feel a little better. I decided make them a special snack, hoping that will smooth things down a bit.

While we're sitting at the table, Paul returned home and kept walking in and out of the kitchen. I get up and go into the bathroom. When I was in the bathroom I can hear Paul talking very loud, I hurry out and ran into the kitchen to see what was going on. Paul has taken all of the food out of the pots and piled it on my son's plate. My son trying to get up, Paul kept pushing him back down into his chair screaming at him.

"I want you to eat it all and you better not get up!"

Pushing Paul away I told my children to go into the living room. Paul standing there looking at me as if he wants to tear me apart. Walking into the living room I ask my children what went on in the kitchen. My daughter told me that she offered my son some of her food and Paul just went off. Seconds later, Paul passes through the living room looking at me and my children rolling his eyes then went into the bedroom. My children not knowing how to take Paul gets up and goes into their bedrooms. I then lay on the couch to watch television. Later I am being awaken by Paul kissing me on my cheek – I pretend to be asleep. Waiting for a few minutes I open my eyes and he's sitting in a chair across from me staring me in the face. I get up off the chair and go into the bedroom, and there he is following right behind me. As he gets closer to me I ask him not to touch me. He then gets in bed and goes to sleep.

Christmas Eve came around, my children and I are so excited, but I still have a little more Christmas shopping to complete. While getting dressed my sister pulls into the driveway. Upon coming inside she informs me that my grandfather passed away, so my children and I immediately got our things together and leaves for my mother's house.

Before my grandfather's death had taken place, Paul and I had planned to go get a few things for my children after work. After receiving the news I call Paul on his job. He lets me know that he will meet me as soon as he gets into town. I then go and visit a few of my friends. It is now 12:00pm and there's no sign of Paul. I call his job once more to see if he's still there, but at this time I do not get an answer. Figuring he's working out of town, I go shopping without him. While on my way back to my mother's house hoping Paul will be here. But once I arrived, I then asked around if anyone has heard from him, but no one seen him.

Well, the sun is beginning to go down and my children are now ready to go home. After telling them I have somewhere to go and that I will take them home as soon as I return, I leave the house to walk to the store. On my way I run into another female that knows my man, she takes me to this house where he is hanging out at. As I walk into the house and seeing the look on his face, he was so startled as if he had seen a ghost.

"Look, I am only here for your half of the money."

"Babe, I got off from work . . . I went by the house and put the money in the dresser drawer."

"Well, the children and I are leaving to go home."

"Okay, I will be home shortly, if I don't get there before you will."

Soon after getting home I get my children settled in for the night, I then went into the bedroom and looked in the drawer. I should have known better, and not to my surprise there's no money. At this moment, I can't even get upset.

Now I am sitting here waiting for Paul to come home, thinking after telling Paul about my grandfather he would've been here with me and the children. It's 6:00am in the morning and Paul is just getting to the house. He's outside now knocking on the door. When I open the door, he's standing here pretending to be so cold; shivering and pleading for me to make him a hot bath. I stood there looking him in the face – wanting so badly to say something, but the words would not come out of my mouth. I go into the bedroom and sit on the bed thinking is this really happening. I then go into the bathroom and run his bath for him, but filling the tub with only hot water. Paul then comes into the bathroom pulling off his clothes and getting into the tub.

While Paul is in the tub I go into the kitchen to start breakfast. A few minutes later, Paul comes into the kitchen and sits at the table and begin acting like he's crying. I trying not to pay him any attention, but my heart won't allow me to ignore him. So I turned around and asked him.

"What is wrong with you?"

Paul looking at me. "Can I hold you in my arms?"

Walking to where he's sitting he reaches out his hand, I then reached out my hand towards him; he clasped it with his and pulls me closer to him and sits me on his lap without saying a word. We are just staring each other in the face, hoping that the love is still there.

"I don't want to hear anymore lies."

But I never bothered to ask about the money or his where about, because at this point in time, it wasn't about the money, it's about my family and our relationship.

I then get up off his lap and go into the bathroom. While standing here for a few minutes still thinking about making another go at this, I turned on the faucet and refreshed myself by wetting my face. Then I go back into the kitchen to complete my breakfast.

Hours much later, Paul begins to make dinner. While dinner is cooking, my children and I are sitting around watching television. Minutes later, dinner is done – we all sit the table laughing and talking; having a pretty good time. We all talked about our day, and afterwards Paul was a little tired and went to bed leaving me and the children up watching television.

Once Paul closed the door of our bedroom, all of a sudden, both of my children look me in my face . . .

"Mom, we are not understanding you. You sit here and let this man tell you anything, . . . and you believe it!"

Looking at the two of them, knowing what they could be feeling right now I said, "It is going to be alright."

They both looked at each other – not saying a word, got up and headed to their bedrooms, leaving me here by myself.

As I was laying on the couch to gather my thoughts, I must of drifted because of exhaustion (*getting very little rest*) because while doing so I fell asleep. Hours later I am being awakened by Paul, requesting that I join him in bed. I then got up and went with him into the bedroom and we both called it a night.

A few days later I returned back to work only having to work three hours, but I hoping for more, my hours went by very quickly and it's time to go home. Upon getting into the house the dinner was already made and there's a dozen of roses on the table with a note which reads, 'I will see you after work.'

Being that I have errands to run I put my food away and leave the house. As I get into town I run into one of Paul's friends. He calls me over to the side saying to me that he and Paul had a talk one day, and Paul told him that he's going to stop having dinner with us; that he doesn't want to sit at the dinner table with me and my children. He said it's because he hates looking into my children faces. My mouth dropped wide open and I can't say nothing. I was deeply in shock from what he had told me.

I immediately returned home only to find Paul sitting in the living room. I then called my children out of their rooms for dinner just to see if Paul is going to join us. While he's still sitting there, I walk up to him and asked him to come join us in the kitchen. I said to myself, "Will you just look at this *Mother Blanket* here!" There he is sitting here trying to pretend like he's watching television. At this point now, I know his friend wasn't making something up. So after me and my children went ahead and finished our dinner without him, they decided to go to their bedrooms while I finished cleaning up the kitchen.

Once I got done, I left the kitchen and headed into the bedroom and laid across the bed – hoping that this so-called man of mine would come into the room and say anything foul to me.

And guess what, seconds later he comes in looking at me and asks, "Do you have a problem?!"

Wanting to say what's really on my mind I have to think about my children's feelings, and also in order not to cause one.

I quickly then responded "No," and then said, "I hope you don't cause a problem." He stood over me for a minute with this irritated look on his face, then turned himself around and exited out the room. Once I knew that he was completely out, I then fell asleep.

YEAR

1 9 9 6

Chapter
16

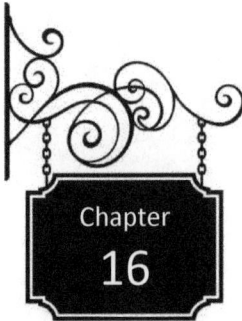

Its January 1st, we all have to get up early. It's the day my grandfather is being laid to rest. Before getting dressed Paul says to me, "I would like for you to get my clothes together because I have a job to do, and I will meet you at your mother's house."

I begin to get this gut feeling that he's not going to show up. My children and I went ahead and got dressed to leave the house anyway. A few minutes later my sister arrives to pick us up. After getting in the car she asks "Where's Paul?" Explaining to her that he has a job to go do, and he will be meeting us at the house. she then gives me this funny look. Shortly we arrived at my mother's house only to find everyone else still getting dressed to leave to go to the church. Now I'm sitting here wondering will Paul make it in time. Ten minutes before leaving Paul finally shows up. Because of the shortage in time, he has to rush to get dress.

After the funeral service we all return to my mother's house for the eating – noticing Paul is trying everything that he knows on how to get away.

I said to him, "If you leave this house, I am not coming home tonight."

Paul, staring me in my eyes and replied, "So what? . . . Do you have plans to do something else?"

I stared right back into his face and said, "Leave and you will see."

Two hours later, we left to go home and relax. We arrived home and got undressed and made ourselves comfortable. While sitting around, I noticed Paul continued to watch the clock. He said that he is going to walk next door to talk with the neighbor. Before leaving out of the house I ask for all of the money out of his pockets and his wallet. Believe it or not, he gave them to me. I took the money, his wallet, and put it in my purse.

While Paul standing here *like a lost child* looking at me in my face. I said to him, "You can leave now." He started to look up at me, but then he just shook his head walked out of the house.

Later that evening, I am hearing voices outside my living room window. I get up and go to the door and there's some people walking out of my yard. By now its dark out and I cannot see who they are. Minutes later Paul comes into the house not saying a word to anyone, instead he goes directly into the bedroom. All of a sudden I am hearing him moving things around the room as if he's looking for something. I continue to watch television because I know he's looking for the money. He then walks out of the room and stands in the hallway.

"Hey babe, can you come here for a moment?"

I know what he wants, but I'm not giving it to him . . . "No!"

"Why not?"

I just kept silent – not giving him any response. He again walks right back out of the house, this time slamming the door behind him.

After Paul leaves I went ahead and locked the doors behind him. I rush to the living room window only to see Paul sitting on the porch talking to himself. I then close the curtain and went into the bedroom. As I started to get in the bed, he's pounding on the door as if there's something wrong with him. I get up to go and open the door. After doing so, I went back to my room and jumped right into bed. As I was starting to get some rest, I just kept wondering what is going to happen next. Sure enough, moments later here comes Paul finding his way into our room and slides into bed; lying beside me, takes my hand and puts it up against his face and begin kissing the palm of my hand.

I then pull my hand away.

Now I am lying here with tears in my eyes hoping that he does not start an argument. Instead, he gets up off of the bed murmuring to himself and walks out of the room. I tiptoed to the open doorframe of our bedroom to see where he's going. There he was, laying on the couch fast asleep.

It is now income tax time I am so tired of walking or having to find a ride to my mother's house I decide to buy a car. I go into town to this man that has a garage shop with a few used cars. After telling him my problem he offers me a car for the price of $750 dollars. I had no choice, . . . I went ahead and bought it!

So happy to finally have a car I hurry home so that I can take my children for a ride.

Upon pulling into the driveway Paul comes outside opens my door and says to me "I like our car!"

Looking at him and saying to myself, "Oh now it is our car. How much money have you put into this."

But trying not to start a fight and wanting to make this work I say to him, "On the days I don't have to go to work I will allow you to use the car. But, . . . under one condition – that you do not ride any of your friends in the car."

After getting out of the car Paul asks if can he take the car for a test drive, saying to myself already he's about to pull the smartest tricks on me. A few hours had gone past, Paul pulls into the yard in the car; he has one of my brother's with him. After getting inside he says to me that he went by my mother's house and my brother asked if he could ride with him to visit me and my children. My brother comes inside and sits down only for a short period of time and now he's ready to leave. I told Paul to please take him straight home and bring my car back because as of now he's not added on the insurance.

As soon as Paul leaves the house the landlord pulls into the driveway. I go outside to speak with her there and then she tells to me that she's giving me a two weeks' notice, and we need to find another place to stay because her son is ready to move back home and the house really belongs to him. At this point I really cannot say a word, it's like someone just kicked me in my stomach. Returning back into the house I break the news to my children, but not knowing where we are going to go because there's no more houses in the surrounding area.

My children said to me, "Hey Mom, maybe we can move back in with grandma."

"I'm so sorry children, but there's not enough room for everyone."

They both say to me, "Well, you stay with Paul and let us live with her."

I replied, "You guys are my children."

My daughter jumps up out of her chair and runs down the hallway screaming, "I don't want to live with him!"

I go into her room to calm her down – letting her know that maybe things will get better, and that she just might meet some friends. She calmed down a bit once I told her this.

As Paul walks through the door I ask him to have a seat I then break the news to him. He says to me that it is not over and that he will find a place for us to live. After getting into bed I let Paul know that this really has to stop because it is really upsetting my children. Before we called it a night, he held me and let me know that it will get better.

The following day I am off from work and there's nothing to do. With time on my hands I decided called one of my friends to come pick me up so I can find another place to live. After hanging up the phone with her Paul pulls into the driveway requesting that I ride with him. Upon getting into the car he says to me that he found a house only a few miles away from my mother. We get to this big house, but as soon as we pulled into the driveway I noticed that the house looked like a barn. We get out the car and look through the living room window. The inside is very huge. By not being able to look upstairs I then begin to wondering what it is like. All of a sudden Paul asks, "Would you like to live here?" Saying to him that I really don't have a choice, but he goes on to say that will be picking up the keys tomorrow. After returning home I tell my children to start packing their things.

While they are getting their things together Paul and I begin talking things over. He says to me that since He will no longer be around the people and the stuff that they do that makes him want to do it, he can really do better. He goes on to say that he promises he is going to change his ways because he wants us to stay together forever. We are now moving again!

We once again moved our things room by room. While Paul is moving our things I am setting up the house. at first I get the wrong impression but the house is bigger and more beautiful on the inside. Everyone loves where they are being placed. Paul, my daughter and I are upstairs and my son has his own room downstairs. After getting settled in together Paul and I make a light dinner. Minutes later we all sit down to eat. While eating, Paul excuses himself from the table he then goes into the bathroom and runs the tub with hot water, he then yells for me come into the bathroom. After getting inside he says to me to take off my clothes. While I get undressed he goes back into the kitchen to check on my children. After doing so he returns back into the bathroom and takes off his clothes. We both finally begin to relax. He then slides behind me and takes me in his arms – still promising to start a whole new beginning. Looking up at the door while soaking in the bathwater I say to him "You have to show me this." After relaxing for a while we get out of the bathtub and got dressed, went upstairs to our room and end the night.

Days have now gone past, things are now beginning to look a little better . . . so I thought.

After returning home from work there's a note on the table that says 'I have a surprise for you.' I go upstairs into the bedroom to look for the surprise but there's nothing here. I then go back downstairs to get my car keys and leave the house to pick up my children from the bus stop. On the way home I ask my children, "How were you guys day at school?" In response, they both told me that it was okay for now. We get to the house and go inside, there's Paul standing on the bottom step to the stairway requesting that I come into the bedroom. After getting into the bedroom Paul goes to sit on the bed requesting that I come closer to him. I then go and stand in front of him. He gets up takes a box out of his pocket and says to me that he wants me to sit in the rocking chair. He then opens the box. To my surprise it's a diamond cocktail ring. He places the ring on my finger then hands me the receipt. Upon looking at it I am speechless! Tears begins to flow down my cheeks . . . for every tear that falls, Paul kisses me on my cheek.

After having our moment together, I go downstairs to help my children with their chores so that we can go meet the neighbors. While doing so Paul prepares the meal. We walk around the neighborhood to introduce ourselves to everyone. Upon doing so we are becoming tired and my children are ready to return home, we then go back to the house. As we walk through the door Paul has the table already set, being that the kitchen is so huge we have a table on both sides of the room. It's time for us to get cleaned up for dinner.

Paul and I sat at one table while my children sits at the other. I am feeling so strange not being able to sit at the table with my children because I have always eaten with them. While eating, my children and I have to talk about our day from across the room in between Paul giggling and continuing to give us all funny looks. I have to admit that it was funny. After we were all done eating my children excused themselves from the table. Leaving Paul at the table I get up and begin to clean the dishes, Paul excused himself also and went upstairs. After finishing my cleaning, I too went upstairs. Paul says to me to relax for a little while and let my children get prepared for the following day.

One hour later I am lying on the bed trying to fall asleep, Paul pretending that he has forgotten something and that he has to leave the house for a few minutes. After leaving the house I go downstairs to run me a bath of hot water, put in a few drops of bubble bath, put my scented candles around the tub and then got in. While relaxing Paul pulls back into the driveway. Hearing the car door slam I get out of the bathtub and get dressed before Paul can make it inside. After my bath I go into the living room and laid on the couch. Paul comes inside asking, "Why did you take a bath without me?" When I told him that it's because I didn't know what time he had planned on returning, he looks at me and then walks away. Still laying on the couch I became so relaxed that I fell asleep.

Chapter
17

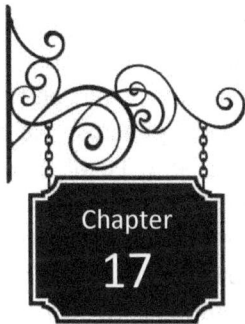

It's Valentine day! I have been looking for Paul to change but he's still being very nice. The way he has been acting really have me thinking even harder about him. On my way home from work I stop by the store to pick up a few things to make something special for dinner. After getting home I go inside to put the things away and there's a note on the refrigerator from Paul that reads, 'Do not cook I am making something special.' I then leave the house to pick up my children from the bus stop. Afterwards, I took them to the store to buy them a gift for today. After making their purchase we returned home. Upon getting inside they begin their homework. Two hours later Paul returns home from work. When he came inside he went straight upstairs gets his changing clothes and came right back downstairs, and jumps into the shower. After finishing he comes and begins to prepare his special meal. Thirty minutes later dinner is being served. We all sat down to eat as always – it's the usual.

After we all finished, Paul gets up and goes upstairs. Wondering what went wrong I go upstairs behind him to find Paul sitting in the rocking chair. I glanced at the bed to see he already had the clothing that he wants me to put on for the night laid across it. Paul then gets up out of the chair and lays me on the bed. As he looks into my eyes I ask myself who is this person, I pick up my clothes off of the bed and then go and get into the shower. I finish and went back upstairs. After getting into the room Paul now gets his things and goes downstairs and gets into the shower. While he's in the shower I laid across the bed and started to feel myself becoming very sleepy. Finally Paul comes back into the room and puts on a movie for the two of us to watch. While watching the movie I fell asleep not knowing how long I have been out. Being awaken by Paul kissing me on my lips . . . let's just say it turned out to be a good night.

A few weeks later it's my first day on a new job not knowing what to expect but it requires me to get home later than I expect to. After getting to work I call Paul asking that if it's not a problem to take a few minutes from work to go home and unlock the door for my children. I continued on with my day as the time is going by very fast, but the drive home seems so long it's like I'm a million miles away. Upon getting home and pulling into the driveway my son walks up to the car and says to me that he doesn't know what's wrong with Paul, but that he's very upset. And that after letting us in the house Paul came inside slamming things around and saying things about my sister and I not paying him any attention. I told my children to go ahead and do their homework while I start dinner. While the dinner is cooking my children and I are sitting around in the kitchen still talking. When Paul walks through the door he looked at my son's head and asks, "Did you comb your hair before leaving for school this morning?"

I said to Paul, "Yes he did."

He looks me in the face and says, "I am not talking to you!"

Saying back to him in response, "I know you are not, but I saw him comb his hair."

Paul then goes into the bathroom gets a comb and comes back into the kitchen stands over my son's head and begins pulling the comb through his hair with force. Seeing the look in my son eyes I snatch the comb out of Paul's hand. As I attempt to make my son get up out of the chair, Paul pushes me away trying to defend my son. I walk up to Paul and give him a big push. Paul pushes me again, this time a little harder. We then begin to fight. I sent my children to their rooms. As I begin to walk out of the backdoor to the carport, Paul pushes me from behind. I then fall on the concrete not being able to get up Paul comes charging towards me and stands over me. My daughter now standing in the doorway with a knife in her hands.

"Paul if you hit my momma again I am going to stab you!"

At this point Paul and I both are looking into her eyes, she has a very serious look on her face.

Paul begin yelling at her to put the knife away but she starts walking toward him knowing that she will hurt him – I beg her to put the knife away. My daughter still standing holding the knife Paul walks away from the house. Me being in so much pain I crawl to the steps asking my children to help me inside of the house. I get inside and laid on the couch not wanting my children to see me cry. I fought to hold back the tears but letting them know that I am okay. Minutes while lying on the couch Paul comes inside looking me and then goes upstairs to get his night clothes and went into the bathroom to take a shower. I'm trying very hard to force myself to get up from this couch because I really don't know what is going to happen next. Paul finally gets out of the shower and walks pass me as if I am not here and leaves me on the couch. My children willingly come out of their rooms to help me upstairs, but being in so much pain I cannot move.

Early the next morning I called out from work because the pain has now gotten worse. After getting dressed I take my time and makes it to my neighbor's house to get her to take me the hospital. After getting there my neighbor and her husband helped me out of the car and inside. Being examined, I find out that I have three fractured ribs and a bruised hip. I return home to find Paul and my children inside waiting on me, Paul looking at me asked, "What did the doctor say about your condition?" Telling him what was said he just looked at me without any remorse. After a brief talk he gets up and goes into the kitchen to start dinner. One hour later he calls everyone to the table but I cannot move, so my daughter brings my food to me. I finish my food and tried to make my way upstairs. I finally made it into the bedroom and laid across the bed, and after taking a pain pill I end up falling asleep.

Upon being awakened by the man who wants to marry me but yet beats me, he gets my night clothes and help me downstairs to the shower. While in the shower I start to think 'Is it really worth it?' I finished in the shower and head back upstairs, then laid back into bed while he sleeps in the rocking chair.

A few days later I still cannot move around like I really want to, all I can do is lay around in pain and cry. Somehow one of my girlfriends heard about what had happened, so she comes by to pay me a visit. Upon coming inside she notices that I can barely walk.

She says, "Tell me what happened to you." Explaining to her she stops me and says that she has been around people who have drug problems, and when they cannot get a fix they get very angry and take it out on the nearest person closest to them. She goes to say that I need to leave because it is only going to get worse.

I said to her with concern, "I have no place to go."

Before leaving she looks at me and says, "You need to be careful of Paul," and then walks out of the house.

Trying very hard not to dwell on the conversation my girlfriend and I just had I put it all to the back of my mind because my children are finally home from school, and I need to help them get prepared to go to my mother's house. While my children are getting prepared to leave their ride pulls into the driveway. After saying our goodbyes they leave the house. Paul leaves the house also, not having a clue to where he is going I go and laid back down on the couch. Later Paul returns home with a dozen of roses; he has six whites and six reds, he then sits on the chair next to me and puts his arms around me and planting kisses on my forehead – telling me how much he loves me. He then goes on to tell me what happened to him in his past relationship as if I haven't heard it all before. I am not giving any respond because I really don't feel like arguing, so for the rest of the evening and night I am going to speak very lightly.

Today started out very calm and quiet, Paul and I decided to go pick up the children from my mother's house. We get to my mother's to find one of my brother's ex-girlfriend is here to visit. After getting out of the car we go inside of the house to talk with my mother. We were all just sitting around talking until all of a sudden we hear a whole lot of loud talking and cursing coming from the outside, we rushed to the door to see my brother screaming at his former girlfriend trying to get her to go home. She's standing in the middle of the street with her shirt and bra off. Then suddenly out of nowhere she turns her back towards everyone standing in the yard and pulls her pants and panties down. While standing next to me Paul looking and talking dirty about my brother's girlfriend, but I am not saying a word . . . I just walk away.

Paul comes into the house asking me why I'm mad, I tried to tell him that I'm not but he kept insisting that I was. I told him that I'm ready to go home, and that we need to get the children and leave. Whether he agreed or not, we all got in that car and left. On our way home everything seems to be going good, but as soon as we get closer to the house Paul starts an argument.

"I'm not going to argue with you Paul, in front of my children."

"Stop the car!"

"No, . . . I am not!"

As I then begin to pull the car into the yard Paul opens

the door and jumps out of the car. After driving under the carport to park the car Paul walks up.

"Did you see what your mother did? She pushed me out of the car!"

Trying to explain to my children, "No, I did not push him out of the car!"

Paul constantly yelling, "You're a liar! . . . Liar, Liar!"

My children and I then get out of the car and go inside. Paul still wanting to start an argument, but I am refusing to do so. Paul then grabs the car keys and storms out of the house, my son standing with this look on his face says to me, Mom, he's going to find your brother's girlfriend."

Okay now that's something to think about.

Thirty minutes later the girl that lives around the corner from me stops by, I hurried to the door before she could get out of her car and asked her to take me to find my car. She says, "Let's go."

We all get into her car and went to my mother's house, but he's not here. So we began riding around town to find him. Finally, we run into him – he has one of my brother's and some other people in my car.

"Paul, I want you and everyone else to get out!"

Paul getting upset begins cursing at me. At this point, I don't care upon getting into my car . . . I noticed my vents are pulled out, the knobs on my radio are gone, and there are footprints on my car pocket. All I can do is sit here and look at my car.

Saying to my girlfriend, "Please follow me home."

We get to the house and go inside. My girlfriend sat here staring at me as if I was insane. I already know what she's about to say . . .

"Are you crazy?! Shaking her head and slapping her hands on the top of her thighs in discuss. "Why are you going through this?"

"I really love him and I promised to help him get better."

I don't think she wanted to hear that – she got up and just walk out of the house without looking back.

The day after I get up to go outside to warm the car, still mad from the night before. In the meantime, I'm not saying anything to Paul about it.

After seeing my children off to school I leave and go to my mother's house and stay with her for a little while. Thinking Paul is at work I go home. After getting home I go upstairs to find Paul in bed asleep. I tiptoe back downstairs and go outside to wait on my children to get out of school. Later this afternoon two of my brother's and one of their girlfriends comes by to visit. Paul wakes up and decides to put some meat on the grill.

We all start out having a good time until all of a sudden my brother's girlfriend go inside of the house, but it just seems like she was taking such a long time to return back outside. I then go inside to see if she's okay, lo and behold, she's in the kitchen pouring dish liquid over the dishes that's in the sink. I walk up to her ask her very nicely and asked her to leave out of my kitchen. She says to me that she's not leaving. I then go back outside and asked my brother to get her out of my house, Paul intervenes and asks me why does she have to leave out when my other brother is sitting in the house.

After my brother's girlfriend comes out of the house she begins dirty dancing in front of my children. Telling her that she needs to leave my home she begins cursing at me. My brother gets upset and begins pushing her out of the yard.

Paul looks at me and says, "Why are you starting a fight?"

After telling him that I am not, he pushed me – I pushed him back.

He then pushes me to the ground, laying here for a second I get up and punch him in the face. I turn to walk away he continues to hit me in the back. I then picked up a stick and begin swinging it wildly to protect myself. While the stick was going back and forth in full motion, Paul being so belligerent (aggressive) walks into it. The stick hits him right on the side his head . . . by accident. In panic mode, I dropped the stick and runs into the house. As both of my children are going to their bedroom, I hear them laughing about how my brother was fighting with his girlfriend. A few minutes later Paul comes inside, but we're saying nothing to each other. He lays on the couch and I go upstairs to the bedroom as usual, and we both called it a night.

The next morning Paul and I both get up early, I go downstairs to sit on the couch. While sitting here Paul comes and goes into the bathroom, he then calls me to come inside with him. We're standing here looking into the mirror at each other.

He asks, "What did we do to each other last night?"

I explained to him what had happened and he looked at my face and says that my left eye is blue. Looking back at him I says to him that his right eye is blue. He then pulls me close to him – kissing my eye and saying to me 'why are we hurting each other,' saying to myself *I wish I knew the answer.*

Paul left for work, but I called out from work because I don't want anyone to see me this way. I got dressed and left the house to go pay my mother a visit. As I go into her house I am hoping no one pays my eye any attention. All of a sudden the question came out.

"What happened to you? You can't hide it!" asked my mother.

I can't lie to my mother, so I told her the whole story.

My mother says to me, "Why are you letting Paul beat on you?" she goes to say, "You better not let him put his hands on my children, . . . because if he does it will be you, me and Paul!"

All I can do is sit here and cry.

Looking me in the face she says, "There's no need to cry, because I means every word I say to you!"

After my mother and I had our little talk, I left to go

home. On my way home I stop by Paul's job to see if he needs anything while I am going to the grocery store. He reaches in his back pocket and gives me all the money that he has in his wallet saying to me in confidence that I already know what to buy. I go to the store and picks up the things that I need, including Paul's beer then I left to go and pick my children up from the bus stop.

My son gets in the car and says to me, "Mom, you are so dumb!"

I looked at him and said, "I am not going to allow you to talk to me this way, I know how you are feeling."

I am now beginning to see the change in my children's attitudes, they are getting very upset with Paul for treating me the way that he is and they are upset with me for allowing it to happen. They are now saying negative things about him. Trying to explain to them that it was wrong because he is an adult, and that I will not let him hurt them.

Hours later Paul comes home from work, my children and I are sitting outside enjoying the afternoon. Paul walking pass us as if we do not exist again, goes into the kitchen and sits at the table. A few seconds later Paul begins making a strange sound. As I run into house there he is lying on the floor having a seizure. I yell to my children to come inside, telling them to go up the street and get the EMS.

My son standing here asking, "Why should I go?"

I am pleading for him to just go – he goes outside and stands in the driveway instead. My daughter then runs out of the house and heads down the street to get them. Minutes later the EMS arrives, Paul is now up and sitting at the table. I then call his mother requesting that he goes to the hospital, but he refuses to go. Paul now can't explain what happened to him, he makes me feel so guilty saying if only we wouldn't have had that fight last night. After settling down for the night I am trying to figure out what could have happened to Paul, but he kept on insisting that I go to sleep.

Days later I thought after what happened to Paul would have made him changed but it hasn't, he has now started nitpicking with my children. I go to pick my mother up to spend the day with us, when we get to the house Paul has a fire burning in the backyard; he's just finding things to burn. Paul and I are back to not saying nothing to each other. My mother and I walked pass him and gone into the house while leaving my children on the outside. A few minutes later my mother decides to go back outside to sit and talk with Paul. All of a sudden I am hearing the two of them arguing. I hurried outside to see what is going on, my mother says to me while she was talking to Paul he fell asleep, so she told my children to go play. After they got of the yard she played a trick on Paul to wake him up.

She said, "I started yelling to him, 'Paul wake up because the fire has gotten out of control!' he then jumps up and goes down the street to get your son. As they both walked into the yard Paul begin arguing at him." She goes on, "He then picks up a board and attempt to hit your son with it. I told Paul that if you to hit my grandson with that board, I will knock your ass out!"

My mother is now very upset and she's ready to leave, but before leaving she says to Paul, "I want you to hit him . . . and I will be coming back!"

On my way taking my mother home she says to me that I need to get my children away from him before he hurts one of them. I said to her "Where am I going to go with two children? Your house is already full of people . . . and please don't worry so much."

My children and I get back to the house, we go inside and begin packing our things having almost gotten everything out of the house. Paul comes inside pleading that we do not leave. So upset, I begin to cry. My children begging me to leave. So we got in the car and left to go find a place for us to live. Riding around for hours and hours, and still no luck. Upon returning home my children gets out of the car and goes inside while I get our things from the car. So happy for us to be back at home Paul comes outside to help me bring our things back inside, but for the rest of the evening my children and I try to make the best of it by staying away from Paul.

A week later, I woke up early to get my children prepared for school. I go downstairs to wake my son up and noticed that he's not in his room. I am thinking that he has already left to go to the bus stop. After my daughter gets dressed, I then leave to take her to the bus stop, but to my surprise my son is not here. After leaving my daughter I went back to the house to find Paul waiting on his ride for work. As I walk into the house he asks me have I dropped my children off yet, saying to him yes and in returns I asks, "Why do you ask?" He says to me because he came downstairs earlier this morning and your son wasn't in his room. Trying not to worry, I go on with my day hoping that my son went to school.

Hours has now passed, it's time for me to pick my children up from the bus stop. My daughter told me that he wasn't on the bus, nor was he in school today. At this point, I am really becoming nervous thinking that he has ran away from home. I walked over to my neighbor's house explaining to her my situation and asking if she give can give me a ride to my mothers. As we arrived in my mother's driveway, I jumped out of the car and ran inside to talk with my mother about what had taken place. She looks directly at me and said, "You better find him and I mean find him fast!" My neighbor and I left my mothers and went to the police department to file a missing person report. At this point I have no other choice but to call Paul. In a panic I make the call. I told him that I cannot find my son and I don't know where he may be. He said that he will take some time off and help me.

After returning home a few hours later I received a phone call from my mother saying to me that she has just seen my son passing through town riding in an 18-wheeler truck. I was so happy to receive the news I begin to cry. Minutes later Paul arrives home asking if there were any luck finding my son. I told him that he should be on his way home because my mother just called about five minutes ago and that he's in a truck heading this way. Paul then says to me that if he was his mother, he would break his neck. I say to him *'that will not happen'* and I walk away. From the comment given to Paul he gets upset and leaves the house, my son then walks through the backdoor almost at the exact same time. I was so excited to see him I began asking him questions to find out what caused him to do such a thing and why.

Hearing his side of the story he says to me, "Mom, I got suspended from school and I didn't wanted to tell you because I knew you was going to say something to Paul about it, and just knowing – he was going start something with the two of us. So while standing at the bus stop a guy I know came by and asked me to ride with him. And when I knew that I couldn't come back home, I just went with him."

Explaining to him that I am going to punish him for what he has done, my son tries to make me feel guilty by saying that I am only going to punish him because Paul told me to do it. Thinking about it for a minute I have no choice but to go through with the punishment in order for my son to learn not to keep anymore secrets from me.

After everything blows over my children and I begin to settle down while talking about how our day went, all of a sudden Paul comes downstairs and becomes angry because I am sitting here talking with them. Upon leaving out of the house, he slams the door while walking out. At this point I really don't care anymore about him leaving the house, my children and I then got prepared for the next day, and then head off to bed – not knowing if Paul is going to return or not, . . . it didn't matter. I am now tired and I'm getting some sleep.

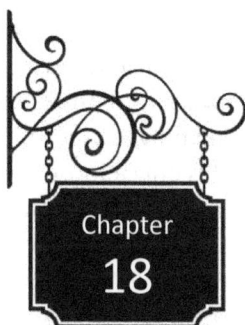

Chapter
18

It's Thanksgiving Eve, me and Paul's 2nd anniversary of being together. While getting up early to get our day started Paul decides to go shopping while my children are still asleep. While walking around in the store a strange man walks up to the two of us and gives Paul $20 dollars, he then says to the two of us you guys looks so lovely together. In my mind I am saying 'if only you know what is hiding behind that smile.' After getting the things we need, we headed back home, and on our way Paul says to me, "I am going to do something different. I've decided not to make dinner . . . we're going to have a cookout instead." We returned home get everything out of the car and go inside. Paul requests that I go and pick up my mother and other family members while he prepares the food. I pick up everyone and return home.

As soon as I walk through the door Paul takes the car keys and leaves the house. Everyone looking at me as if to say he invites us here and then he leaves the house. While getting things prepared Paul walks through the door holding a bottle of Champagne and one rose – being so nice, he asks my daughter to assist with the cooking. Throughout the day I am wondering how long this is going to last, luckily Paul is not acting out. After all, it really turned out to be a pretty good day and night moment for us all.

The following morning I get up early because I have to go to work. On my way outside to start the car Paul rushes to the door saying to me that he knows I am working in the town where my best guy friend lives in, and that he knows exactly how much time it takes for to return home. And it is only a forty-five minute drive. Knowing what he is trying to say, I told him that he is never home on time, but he is telling me what time to be at home knowing I am never late. It's just my luck, while on the way to work the car breaks down on the street where my ex-guy friend lives. Having to leave the car on the side the road and walking to my job. After getting there, I call Paul to see if he will pick me up after work and check out the car, He tells me that he will be there as soon as he can get a break. Three hours later Paul shows up. After getting into the car, he begins cursing at me because of the location where the car is parked. Trying to explain that's my only way to work he says to me that he don't want to hear that.

As we get to the car Paul continues cursing at me. I am sitting here in this truck with all sorts of thoughts going through my mind. He finally gets the car started. Before getting ready to leave, in a harsh way he says to me that he wants me to go straight home. In order not to argue I get in the car and drive off. Forty-five minutes later we arrive at home. After getting inside, Paul accuses me for the car breaking down also.

"You only wanted to see if your ex-guy friend would have come to your rescue!"

I go upstairs to the bedroom and shut the door. Paul then leaves to go back to work. Around 6:00pm Paul returns home grabs the car keys and storms out of the house. I'm thinking how is he blaming me for tearing up the car when I very seldom drive my own car. Later Paul returns home high still – along with the cursing. I refuse to say anything back because I know things will get out of hand, so for me it will be a quiet night.

Days later, Paul plans my daughter a last minute sleepover. So he says to me that he promised to do something for her. After getting home from work Paul asked me go and pick up some of her friends while he makes the snacks. To be honest, I am really not up for it, but to make him happy I go and picks up nine girls to attend. Upon returning home and going inside while the girls are getting settled in Paul says to my son that he is not allowed in the living room. Asking Paul what he supposed to do if my son has to use the bathroom knowing he has to come through the living room. Even in this, knowing he's trying to start an argument so he can leave the house and leave me stuck with all the girls, he then says to my son go out through his bedroom window and come through the kitchen door, and if it is locked, for him to hold it. My son looks at me in my face and goes back into his bedroom – Paul goes upstairs.

I also go upstairs, but to just get my things because I am sleeping with the girls. Getting into the room I find Paul sitting in the rocking chair with a funny look on his face. He then gets up and goes downstairs and get the car keys again and leaves the house. My son comes to me saying, "Mom, I started to say something to your boyfriend," in return I let him know that I was so glad that he didn't say anything because he would have showed out in front of these girls.

While the girls and I lie on the floor watching television, Paul comes inside, of course he's high but this time he is in a good mood, so I don't even bother to ask him any questions. We all just call it a night.

It's almost Christmas time and I have lost my job but I will not let it get me down, I am going to make sure my children have a good Christmas. I decide to go get help from this program to get some assistance for a few things for them, including some clothing. It is so sad, I can't even afford to buy a Christmas tree because Paul tells me he don't have that kind of money for any Christmas stuff. By having a rubber tree in my living room before, I decided to use it again. I only have a dollar cash left to spend so

I came to a decision to put up a few lights on the outside. After straightening up the house my children and I go to the store to pick up some lights and a few more things. We returned home and put up the lights around the house which did not last that long because a little girl in the neighborhood came along and cut them in half from the outside. Being so upset, I walk down to the little girl's mothers' house to tell her what her daughter had done to my lights. Just by listening to her talk, it is as if she could care less. Getting home and talking to Paul about the little girl's mother and what she said to me, he looked at me and asked me why am I making such a big deal about these lights. Almost going through the roof I say to my children that it is going to be okay. Paul then makes a comment to me saying that I'm acting like I have little children, that they are too big to be worrying about Christmas. My children remembering what he said from earlier today about not buying them anything for Christmas, they both get up and go to their bedrooms.

After seeing the look in my daughter's eyes I go upstairs to have a talk with her telling her to forget what Paul had said and that she will never get too old for Christmas, and that she will be getting something. I kissed her on the forehead and walked out of the room. Therefore, now upset, I go into my bedroom and lays across the bed not waiting on Paul. I called it a night.

Christmas Eve, I now have to go pick up my children things that they received for Christmas, I get the boxes and take them home, but after seeing everything I want to cry . . . all the toys are so dirty and the clothes are too small. Now I don't know what I am going to do. I then walk to my neighbor's house. After getting inside I tell her about the things I received for my children. She tells me not to worry because she knows of this place where she can take me to get better things. We get to the place there I am being allowed to pick out what I want for my children that I know they will enjoy having. After getting back home I wrap up their gifts and put them under the rubber tree, Paul comes from work asking me the question, "How did you get gifts for your children?" Trying to explain to him the neighbor took me to a place that she knew of, he says to me that he doesn't believe me, and where did I get money from to buy the stuff. By him not hearing a word I'm saying, I rather not turn this into a fight. Later after picking my children up from my mother's house, they were very surprised to see gifts under the rubber tree. I then made a light snack for me and my children to eat and calls it a night.

Christmas Day! Even though without much we are still happy to be alive and well, my children are up and ready to open their gifts. They are so excited for what they have. Really not expecting nothing for myself, to my surprise my daughter made me a gift and my son brought me an ashtray with a cup holder that says *Sip and Smoke.* Telling them their gifts are wonderful it made them feel so good.

We are all getting dressed to go to my mother's house, we arrive to her house and go inside where she's showing off all of her gifts that my other family members had given her. I felt so bad because I didn't have any money to buy her anything. She says to me, "As long as you are here, it's all what matters to me."

Our day goes by pretty well, I really enjoyed my family but the time has passed and now it's time to go home. On our way back to our house, Paul and I are still not saying a word to each other. We get home and everyone couldn't wait to get inside. Paul goes upstairs and sits in the rocking chair by the bed and rolls himself up a joint, and then he comes back downstairs goes outside and smokes it. Once he finished smoking his joint, he then comes back inside wanting to talk, my children took one look at him, got up and went to their bedrooms . . . also not having nothing to say to him. I am just sitting here tired from earlier today, so I get up and go upstairs myself and called it an

evening.

YEAR

1 9 9 7

Chapter
19

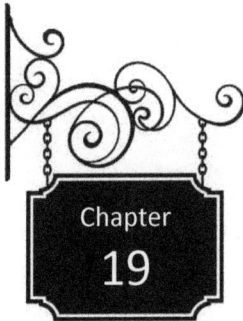

Paul is now summoned for child support court being the amount is very high he really don't know what he is going to do. I have to do what I think is right to do. I begin calling around to some of the lawyers that I am familiar with to get help. Upon talking with one of the lawyers I am being informed to have him at the office at our earliest convenience, we then leave to meet with him. While speaking with the lawyer he informs Paul that he will do all he can do to keep him from going to jail. On the way home, Paul asked for my hand, he then begins telling me how much he loves me. Thinking to myself 'Of all the hell you are taking me and my children through I am here standing by your side.'

Forgetting to leave the door unlocked my children were sitting outside on the porch waiting. Upon pulling into the driveway Paul reaches over and begin to kiss me, both my children looking at me with confused looks on their faces. We get out of the car and we all go inside. Paul saying to me go get some rest and that he will make dinner for us. My children still trying to figure out why am I letting Paul kiss on me. Really not wanting to tell them what is going on because I will have to hear my son say his favorite saying to me which is 'Mom you are going to save him again?' So I have to make up something to tell them to ease things over.

Dinner is now ready. Paul then puts the food on the table but before sitting down. He invites my children to sit at the table with us, he then begins talking to them about their day. They both are sitting here with a surprise look on their faces as if to say 'Who is this man?' sitting here.

A few minutes later Paul dismisses himself from the table, my son then asks the question, "Mom, is your man okay?"

Saying to him, Let's keep this evening quiet . . . we don't need him getting upset."

While my children prepare themselves for the following day I put away the dishes and clean the kitchen. After finishing I went to go take a shower. While Paul is upstairs watching television, I go into the living room and fell asleep on the couch.

Two days later it is Paul's court date. After dropping the children at the bus stop, I returned home to get dress. Not knowing what to think rather Paul is going to jail or coming back home. Hours later we are here in the courtroom and our lawyer going in and speaking with the judge. Minutes later he returns calling Paul to the side saying to him that he has done all that he could do, but Paul need money to pay on his child support. The officer coming out saying to Paul that he has to put him into a holding cell until court is over, then Paul turning to me and letting me know that I have about 30 minutes to get $1,000 dollars or he will have to go to jail. I then run downstairs in the courtroom and begin to make phone calls to see if I can borrow the money.

After being turned down by everyone I then make a call to Paul's boss. He says to me that he will give him the money but I have to come and get it. Running to car I then get on the road, putting my life at risk I drive over the speed limit trying to make it to meet Paul's boss which is 26 miles away. Making it there in 15 minutes, after receiving the money I returned to the courthouse in 10 minutes, and upon running inside and paying the money Paul is now being released. We both are so happy but only for a few minutes. Paul looking into my face and saying, "Don't you never drive that way again, you could have killed yourself or someone else!"

Explaining to him, "You are the one who told me you only had 30 minutes, so I hurried there and back, and now you are yelling at me." We get into the house, tired from this long day I go upstairs and lay across the bed. Paul then comes into the room gets out his cigar box and rolls himself a joint, then go back downstairs. While trying to sleep, Paul comes back into the room not wanting to hear nothing he has to say, but he then says to me that he is very sorry for yelling at me, but that I just made him upset with me. Without saying another word Paul leaves out of the room. A few hours later I am being awakened by Paul holding a plate of food in his hands. Not realizing the time I jumped out of bed, Paul says to me, "You need to relax, it's not late – your children has eaten and they are in their rooms."

Now I am wondering to myself has he said anything wrong to my children while I was asleep. Finishing my food I go downstairs and get into the shower, giving Paul time enough to fall asleep. I took longer than usual getting out of the shower. Once done, I went back upstairs to find Paul fast asleep, and then I went back to bed and call it a night.

It's New Year's Eve and Paul starts a new tradition for the bringing in the year, he calls it the seafood eve night. Paul requesting that I get in contact with my family members and his uncle to invite them to join us. Being that it is a last minute notice, yet I'm still on my way to the grocery store. I also go by and pick up my mother and Paul's uncle while he goes fishing. As the time have passed and it is hours later, Paul and the rest of us return to the house at the same time. We all go inside leaving Paul outside in the yard to clean the fishes. Minutes later Paul comes to the backdoor asking his uncle to come out and sit with him. Meanwhile I am getting the other foods prepared for the night.

My mother then walks to the backdoor to see what Paul

and his uncle are doing, she then turns around towards me saying, "They're out there drinking liquor."

Saying to her in return, "I hope Paul do not show out tonight because he cannot handle alcohol."

She then says to me, "I really want him to start while I am here."

I just left it alone.

By not having much to prepare I am now done and so is Paul with the fishes. Paul and his uncle comes inside while waiting on everyone to arrive to begin frying the fishes. Since no one seems to be coming while sitting at the tables Paul goes ahead and gets into the shower. My children, my mother and I are having a good time talking and having a little fun when suddenly Paul walks into the kitchen, he's just standing here looking. My son asking me for something to eat.

As I am getting up to fix him a plate Paul says to me, "How do you think he can eat before anyone else?"

Not having enough time to say anything, my mother jumps in the conversation and says to Paul, "I am hungry too."

We have been sitting here for a period of time and it don't look like no one is coming, so we are going to eat then. Paul with this dumb look on his face says to her, "You haven't gotten yourself something to eat?"

My mother says in return, "So why can't the children eat?"

He then gives a smart remark.

My mother gets up and fixes herself and my children a plate of food and sits back at the table.

Paul begins walking toward my son cursing saying, "You don't need a dam thing to eat!"

Getting upset my mother saying to Paul, "Wait a minute, . . . my money helped paid for this food, and he's going to eat as much as he wants."

After Paul storms out of the backdoor my mother says to

me, "Hurry up and get me out of here because I will pack my foot so far up Paul's ass, he will not be able to pull it out."

Paul's uncle not having a clue of what have been said, says to my mother, "No one is going to do anything to my nephew!"

She says back to him, "I will do the same thing to you because neither one of you knows who you are messing with!" She goes on to say, "Now my daughter maybe afraid of Paul, but I want him to try and touch one of these children in front of me and you both will be in for it."

In order for this situation to not get out of control I requested that my mother and the children go and get into the car.

While going to get my keys Paul says to me, "You can stay there if you want to."

Looking back at him and saying, "I just might," and walks out of the house.

My mother still upset from the way Paul have been acting she's constantly going on about Paul hitting my children, saying to my son, "When you return home . . . and if he hits you, I want you to pick up something and knock him out with it."

I told my mother, "I am not going to let it get that far."

After pulling into the driveway she says to me, "You just need to be careful," she then goes inside.

Minutes later my children and I return home. We go back into the house to find Paul and his uncle passed out on the couch, so my children went to their bedrooms and I'm about to go upstairs; not even bothering to wake up Paul, because I do not feel like fighting tonight. I'm going to go ahead and call it a night.

Chapter
20

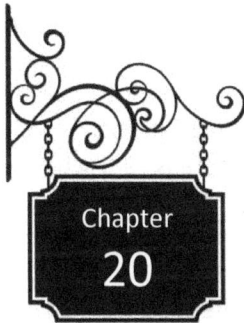

A few months later we are on the move again. As much as me and my children don't want to move away, we have to. Where we're at now is much closer to the school, which is better for them. Also, we're in walking distance to the stores. But again, I have no choice but to move. Being that this is the last minute move we are short of money again. Hating to go to my mother to borrow money, but we really needed $200 dollars to add to the deposit. Upon going to my mother, I have to explain to her the reason for the money, she said to me that she's not giving me her money, but she is loaning it to me and Paul, and that she wants it back because it is his responsibility to make sure that me and my children have a place to stay.

In the process of moving into the home I noticed there's no stove, wondering how are we going to eat. Paul said that we have a grill in the backyard, then he sent me off to the grocery store to buy something that was quick and easy to fix.

After picking up the children from the bus stop we go back to the house. Pulling up into the driveway my children takes a look around at their surroundings and says to me, "Mom, why are we out here in the middle of nowhere?"

"Well, we are far away from civilization and the closest people are two blocks away, but you are closer to a school. While

Paul and his friends finish moving our things, I go ahead and put some meat on the grill while the children are straightening their rooms and other parts of the house. I finished the grilling and then went inside and put away our things. It's becoming late and the sun is beginning to go down, and here is Paul returning to our new home saying that he has gotten everything from the other house, but he has a job that he has to go do, and that he will be returning shortly.

Hours have gone pass and there's no sign of Paul, and being out here without a telephone I have no way of getting in contact with anyone. Being worried, my son comes to me and says, "Mom, you know for yourself Paul is not coming back! Do you not remember who he left with? . . . He left with all the people that smokes crack!"

From being upset and not wanting to say nothing wrong, I just send him to his room. My children then go to bed and here I am waiting on Paul to come home. But I'm trying so hard not to fall asleep. And the thought of being in no man's land . . . What was I thinking? . . .

Hearing noises from the outside I leave out of the bedroom and go into the living room to turn on the television, then laid on the couch – hoping that each car passes the roadway will be Paul. I then get up and check on my children, afterwards I finally fell asleep.

The following morning, Paul hasn't returned home from the night before. My children and I get up and got dressed. Leaving the house I asked my children where they wanted to go. Both said that they wanted to go to grandma's house. After getting to my mother's house I asked her if I can I leave them for a little while so they can to go play with some of their friends. They were so excited . . . saying to me "Yes!" I leave the house and walks to the store, hoping that I will run into Paul on my way there. With having no luck, I continued to the store and then returned to my mother's.

When I got there, I picked up my children and we left to go home. On our way, I am thinking what I am going to say to Paul if he's at the house. As I pull into the driveway I notice the doors are still closed, we get out of the car and go in, but there's still no Paul. My children and I go ahead and put the finishing touches on the inside of our new home. Minutes later a car pulls into the front of the driveway, I go to the door to see who it may be – only to see it's Paul.

Not waiting until he gets inside I ask the question, "Why didn't you come home last night?"

As usual, he comes up with a good lie saying after he finished the job he was doing he went back to the other house to make sure he had gotten everything. And when he was getting ready to leave, the car wouldn't start so he spent the night in the car. By looking him in the face he knows that I am not buying that. I called my children out of their bedrooms, we then walked out of the house and got in the car and left to go back to my mother's.

Upon going back inside she's giving me this funny look – not knowing that my children have already told that Paul didn't come home the night before.

She says to me, "Has he gotten home yet?"

"Who?"

"Earlier, I know you went to look for him."

Trying to explain to her that I didn't, I only dropped my children off so they could spend time with their friends, and while I was here I needed to go to the store. She looking at me as if to say 'close your mouth because I am not hearing you.' All of a sudden she says, "Well, . . . that's on you."

After listening to my mother fuss for a while I get my children and we left again to go back home. When we got into the house, they went straight to their rooms while I prepare something to eat. We still don't have a stove, so I have to do something simple.

My son then comes out of his room and ask, "Where's

the runaway man?"

Saying to him, "In the bedroom . . . and please, let's just keep it quiet because we don't need any trouble out of him tonight, because we are too far away to get help if he shows out."

My children and I then get settled down for the evening I go and take me a shower, afterwards I refuse to go into the bedroom, instead I went into the living room laid on the couch and fell asleep.

Several hours later, I am being awakened by Paul – rubbing his hands on my cheek; telling me that I need to go and get in the bed. I then get up and go into the bedroom. Seconds later Paul comes into the room asking in a harsh way, "Why are you avoiding me?"

Tired and irritated by all this I got snappy. "I am so sick and tired of your lies!" I then plopped myself into bed in frustration and turned my back towards his direction. He then walks out of the room and goes into the living room. All I can say is, "Goodnight!"

Having to get up early – only because I made a promise to my children that I will allow them to spend the weekend with my mother. Before leaving home for work Paul says that he would like for me and my children to return early because this afternoon his boss is having a fish fry at his church around 6:00pm, and he would like for us to attend. Changing the plans for my children, we leave to go spend a little time with my mother. Upset because they both cannot stay the weekend at my mother's house, my children says to me, "Mom, do you really think we are going to the fish fry?" I told them that I really think we will.

Hours later after returning home we're sitting here waiting for Paul to pick us up but it seems as if he's not trying to make it on time. While waiting on Paul his nephew pulls into the driveway and gets out and come inside.

He asks, "Where are your children?"

They are in their rooms."

He goes on to say, "Tell me something, why is it everytime I come here they are in their rooms?" Questioning about it he continues, "This reminds me when I was younger living with my mother and her boyfriend, he would always lock me and my sister in our rooms." He then goes and calls my children out of their rooms to sit in the living room with the two of us.

Minutes later Paul getting dropped off in the driveway, he comes inside and sits on the arm of the couch. I then ask him about what kind of fish is being served at the church. He looked at me all puffy and began cursing at me. I looked back at him and asked in a sneery (scornful) *way because I knew he was lying again*, "What is wrong with you?" Not trying to tell me truthfully what the problem is he just continues to curse.

I get up from my chair and begin to walk off – he too gets up of the arm of the couch walks over to me and begin pushing me. Saying to him, "If you want to leave just go! . . . Because I am not about to argue with you!"

He pushes me again.

All of a sudden Paul's nephew jumps up out of his seat grabs Paul and slams him onto the couch saying to him, "I have had enough Paul!"

Paul then gets up and begin to walk outside, and then once in the yard just kept on walking until he was gone again. Paul's nephew apologizes for his reaction, saying to me that he had a flashback of how it was when he was a little boy. I told him that it was okay. I am just glad he was here, if not it could have turned out to be worse.

After Paul's nephew left the house my children were so amazed of how he threw him on the couch. This seems to be all they can talk about, it was the highlight of the evening.

"Wow, he had a flashback and slammed Paul! But Paul needed a reason to leave the house . . . and looks like he just got it – so that he can go out and get high."

Since we didn't get the chance to go to the church for fish, I decided to make me and my children something to eat, but they only wanted snacks. So we grab us a snack and went into the living room and watch a little television. As the time passes, I tell them to go get some rest – letting them know everything will be okay. Knowing that Paul is not going to return I turned out the lights, and to make my children feel safe I stayed on the couch.

The following morning we are still sleeping. Upon hearing the opening of the backdoor I immediately jump up off the couch thinking that it is Paul. I go into the kitchen to find it is my landlord's husband.

"Excuse me but, why are you in my house at this time of the morning?"

He says to me, "There are a few things that need to be checked out."

Looking at him I said, "You need to leave because Paul is not at home and I don't need anymore problems out of him."

While walking the landlord's husband out Paul walks into the yard asking him the same question I asked earlier. Trying to explain, Paul then turns to the landlord's husband and says to him, "When my woman and her children are here alone, you need to call! . . . You just don't walk into our home." The landlord's husband then leaves the house.

Paul then starts a conversation about him being here, but I am not concerned about him – I am wanting to know where was he last night, but I do not bother to get into it with him. I walk away and go back into the bedroom and get into bed. Paul follows me into the room and lays in bed beside me. He is smelling so bad, I had to find a nice way to get him to clean himself up. So I told him that his clothes smell really bad and that he needs to pull them off and get into the shower.

I thought it would work, but now here comes the lies . . .

He says to me, "Oh, . . . last night? I was at a friend's

house and we all were standing around a fire."

Wanting to ask what kind of fire was he burning to make him smell like raw oysters dipped in chocolate? But I don't want to hear the cursing afterwards. So, while Paul goes and gets into the shower I get out of bed in a hurry and put on my clothing. Minutes later he comes back into the room and ask, "Do you have somewhere to go today?"

Wanting to know why he asked, I replied with . . . "Why?"

He says to me, "Because you are dressed like you are."

Realizing he has been doing drugs all night long, at this point anything will come out of his mouth.

After getting my children dressed also, I take them to my mother's house and returned back home. Now I am standing here trying to figure out a way to stay busy and most of all, stay away from Paul. I then go outside and clean the yard instead. Thinking that Paul is asleep I looked back at the door to see if he's standing there watching me. Unfortunately, he does come outside and sits on the porch – just watching me. I continued with the cleaning hoping that the wrong words don't come out of my mouth so I won't start an argument.

I guess to start a conversation Paul says to me that he will pay the bills in the morning. Wanting to say 'what does that have to do with me,' but Paul continues to talk. At this point I am blocking him out. He being frustrated jumps off of the porch and walks over to me, grabbing me by my arm.

He said, "Will you please stop?!"

I dropped the rake on the ground.

He then offers me to go inside of the house. After getting inside I sit on the loveseat, he then comes and sits beside me – wanting to know what time will my children be returning. I told him that I really don't know. He then asked if he can make love to me. Thinking to myself, 'I know you are not serious when you stayed out all night.' Trying so hard to trust that he wasn't with another woman, and trying to remember his words that he said to me when we first met, '*Whatever I want its already at home,*' while going into the bedroom. I ask the Lord to protect me that I don't come up with nothing. So sick of the excuses, I am so sorry for whatever I've done because I can't even look him in his face.

My children have now returned home. I was so glad to see them walk through the door I asked them how was their visit at grandma's house, but before they can say anything Paul comes out of bedroom, and as usual they get up and go into their rooms to prove a point to Paul. I get up and go behind them. No matter what, I am still going to talk to my children. After speaking with them I call it a night.

We all get up early to get our day started; the children have already left the house for school and Paul left early for work. There's nothing here for me to do so, I decide to get out of the house for a while.

After getting into town I go to the store to play a few games of poker on the machines. Getting into a good game Paul comes into the store. He walks over to where I am sitting.

"Why are you not at home"

"I came to see my mother, but since she is not at home I came here to pass time."

Highly upset he goes and purchases a few items and walks out of the store. After playing a few games I leave to go home. Getting home I go ahead and starts my dinner. It is getting later in the afternoon and my children haven't gotten home yet. I then called the school only to find out that the bus driver drove all the children back to the school and then walked away from the school itself. I have no idea what that was all about, but now I am wondering how my children are going to get home.

Two hours later there is a car pulling into the driveway. Looking out of the door to see it is the bus driver bringing my children home. It must have been a problem with the bus, but I'm glad that the bus driver brought my children home safe.

Thank you, Lord!

After getting inside they sat at the table to begin doing their homework and telling me about their day. Not noticing when Paul came into the yard and knowing he is on the outside, my children are ready to go to their rooms again. Saying to them, "Just sit still." Paul then comes into the house looks at me and my children then walks straight out of the front door. My children and I are sitting at the kitchen table talking. When I looked up, I then saw a puff of white smoke passing across the window. I get up out of my chair and goes to see what's going on. I guess to get out his frustration, Paul went outside and set on the front yard grass (which is that straw some people make brooms with it) on fire. Being that the yard is the size of a football field – the fire has gotten out of control.

I run back into the kitchen informing my children not to come outside. In a panic my daughter runs out to the porch screaming to Paul to put the fire out; the smoke is now becoming very heavy. I run to try and help put the fire out because the smoke is interfering with the vision of the people passing by.

While fighting the fire, we noticed an airplane flying above us, then all of a sudden a fire truck arrives but it is on the opposite side of the road. The more we fight the fire the wider it spreads, people are now beginning to pull off the road at this point. The fire truck pulls into our driveway, the fire chief gets out of the truck and walks over to the two of us asking the question, "Who started the fire?" Paul tries to explain that he was burning the straw to cut the yard. The fire chief goes on to explain to us that he can charge us up to $500 dollars, but we are very lucky – only because we have the proper tools to keep it away from the woods. So they went ahead put out the fire for us and then leaves.

Paul wondering who could have called the fire department, I said to him that it may have been one of the people that were passing by. But I know it had to have been one of my children. Resting on the porch for a few minutes, Paul looks at me and asked, "What do I think about the yard now?" Not saying a word, I get up and go inside of the house and get my things prepared to get into the shower.

After taking a good hot shower my children and I get prepared for dinner, Paul then comes inside still giving my children a strange look. I said to them both "Do not pay him any attention." By not looking him in the face, Paul turns and goes into the bedroom. After having dinner we all called it a night.

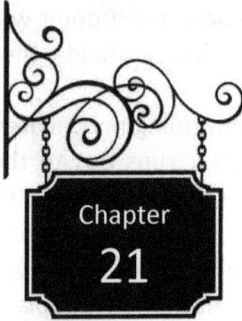

Chapter 21

The following morning upon getting out of bed I receive a call requesting that I report to work. After we all got dressed and on our way leaving out of the house, I tell Paul to meet me at my mother's house because my children wanted to spend some time with some of their friends, and I only have a few hours to work. However, my plans are to meet my children there.

Hours later I am now off from work. I am only a few blocks away from my mother's house, so I decide to walk. After I get to my mother's I asked her if she has seen Paul since I been at work. She told me that she hasn't seen him at any time today. I then go and get my children so we can head home, but we have no way of getting there, so I went to Paul's uncles' house to ask to borrow his car. After picking up the car, I stop back by my mother's to get my children.

As they come out to get in the car one of my brothers said to me, "I am going and spend the night with you guys."

Upon leaving my mother's house I spot Paul sitting on this old lady's porch. I pull over to the side, and into the driveway to find out if he is going home with us. He hops up off of the porch then gets in the car. After he closed the car door, he starts telling me about that the old lady he was sitting up there with told him that I do not care about him, because I am still in love with one of my ex's. He then begins cursing at me saying things that really doesn't matter to me – as I say to him, *"My past is my past."*

Upon speaking on that, my brother's girlfriend just so happens to walk pass . . . now that just made the issue even more worse, oh, yes . . . he has seriously struck a nerve! Looking him directly in his face I say to him, "So I guess that is the reason you are starting with me." He then tells me to stop the car and that he's getting out. I stops the car, he gets out, I drives off, . . . That's right, I left his dusty behind standing in the middle of the road – looking like a squirrel who had just lost his nuts.

My children, my brother, and I get to the house. They go inside leaving me to get the groceries out of the car. While doing so, Paul walks into the yard he begins cursing at me again asking, "Why in the hell you left me standing in the road?!"

Saying to him, "Because you got out of the car."

He then reaches in his pocket and pulls out a pistol and points it at me. Attempting to walk away to go inside, he steps in front of me saying, "If you pass by me I will shoot you in the back of your head!"

Showing no fear, I look him in the face and walked right pass him. As I go up the steps he's still behind me cursing. Seeing the pistol, my son gets up to go into his room. I tell him to stay seated because at this point I don't know what Paul may have on his mind.

Realizing what's going on, my daughter begins screaming and crying – saying to Paul, "Don't shoot my mom!"

Trying to get her to be quiet and not to worry, I sent her into the living room with my brother. And not saying a word, my brother is just sitting here. I then go back outside to get the rest of the bags out of the car, Paul still yelling about shooting me. I turned around looked at him and said, "If you kill me I promise you will not go to jail, but you are going to take care of my children until they are grown, and hopefully . . . they make you suffer."

While trying to block Paul out because I have to think of my children, Paul then walks up behind me and puts the gun to my head saying, "If you move I will pull the trigger!"

My brother gets up out of his chair, goes to the front door and just stands there guessing. By now he is wondering what is going to happen next. I am really trying not to say nothing wrong, because at this point I am really thinking 'what if Paul really shoots me in front of my children and how are they going to handle it?' I take my time and slowly walked away and go into the bedroom. Paul then follows me into the room – he puts the gun down and then begins pushing on me.

Now that he has put the gun down I build up the nerves and pushes him back. Hoping and praying that he does not pick up the gun again and hurt me, I grab a hold of him and held him tight. He shook himself around a bit then pushes me off. I then begin hitting him with all my might. He grabs my arms holding them so tight as if he is trying to break them. In order to get away I had push him so hard that he fell through the closet door. I then ran out of the room into the living room, my children sitting quietly not saying a word, my son looking as if he wants to grab Paul. Getting my son's attention, I shook my head at him so that he won't move, nor cause Paul to act a fool and end up killing us all.

Paul finally coming out of the room puts the gun back

into his pocket and walks out the backdoor. My brother goes to the backdoor to see where Paul may have gone. But then he saw something, and his eyes got as big as daylight. My brother comes running back into the living room, looks right at my children and says to them, "Paul is in the backyard digging a hole, and I think he's going to kill your mom and put her in it."

My daughter almost losing it, goes running into her bedroom telling my brother not to do that. While going into her room to calm her down my brother says to my son, "I am going to get your mom some help!" He then leaves the house walking. Watching him leave out of the yard I am beginning to think 'What if I really need him here to witness if something really happens, and what if Paul kills me and my children in this house, . . . and we are in the middle of nowhere?'

Minutes later, Paul comes to the backdoor yelling for me to come outside. By hearing him yelling for me, my children begging – saying to me, "Mom, . . . please don't go outside!" Now I have to try and get them to understand that I am going to be okay.

Upon getting to the door, I stand here for a minute to pull my nerves together I walk into the yard to find Paul standing in a very dark spot. After getting a little closer he looks at me and ask, "What end do you think I need to start a garden?"

I said, "Are you really serious?!"

To be honest, it really doesn't matter . . . I walked away and went back inside.

I called my children together and explained to them that we are going to be okay, and for them to get some sleep. I kissed them goodnight and send them to bed. I then go into the bathroom and ran some hot water so I can take a nice shower. After getting in the shower, Paul comes and gets in with me. Not saying nothing to each other, I hurried and got out. I then go into the living room and lay on the couch – giving Paul time enough to fall asleep.

Minutes later, I tiptoed into the bedroom got the gun and took out all the bullets, then got on top of him and put the gun upside his head saying to him, "I will hurt you if you ever threaten or try to hurt me again in front of my children!"

After begging me to put the gun down I drop it onto the floor. Paul however, jumps out of bed picks up the gun and opened the barrel to find out that there are no bullets it. He then puts the gun in the closet saying to me, "I will get rid of the gun." But the reason for him having it is because I pissed him off and I walk out of the room.

Anyway, as I leave the room Paul follows me again out of the room requesting that I give him the bullets. I told him that I threw them somewhere in the backyard. He just looked at me, rolled his eyes and then goes back into the bedroom.

Here I am lying on the couch with my heart almost beating out of my chest, thinking 'If I go to sleep, will Paul try to hurt me?' Hearing him moving around in the bedroom I sat up on the couch to see what's his next move. Suddenly, I hear him get into the bed, so I stayed up just long enough until I think he's completely asleep. And just for extra measures, I tiptoed back to the bedroom, slightly crack the door open just enough to peek through – only to find that he's fast asleep. With a half a smile on my face *with caution*, I then go back into the living room and return quietly back on the couch to lay down and close my eyes.

YEAR

1 9 9 8

Chapter
22

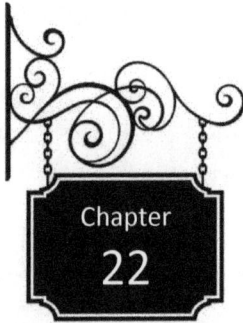

Two years later, it's summertime and it is my weekend to get my niece and nephew. It feels like one of the hottest mornings that we have ever had. Being that Paul has already left for work and I cannot sleep, I decide to go ahead and get my day started. After making breakfast I then awaken my children so they can eat and help with their household chores before Paul returns home on his break.

While on his break and stopping by to grab a bite to eat, Paul asking, "What time are you expecting your niece and nephew to arrive?"

Saying to him, "I really don't know, it could be at any time."

He then grabs himself a beer to drink. After doing so he says to me, "I will see you later this afternoon."

A few hours later my nephew arrives stating that my sister will be coming at a later time. After putting his things away my children were asking about going for a little walk, I gave them the okay and I allowed them to go. Once they left, I began making dinner. Being that it is too hot I decided to make something light and simple.

It is now 3:00pm, the children are finally returning home. We all then go outside and sit on the front porch to try and cool down. While sitting here talking with the children Paul and his nephew pulls into the driveway. As Paul walks into the house the telephone rings. Upon going inside and answering the phone and being that it is so hot I bring the phone outside to talk, it was my niece. She wanted me to know that she changed her mind about coming over to spend the weekend.

Paul comes to the door asking, "Who are you talking with on the phone?"

In reply, "It's my niece."

He then gives me this look, snatches the phone out of my hand and throws it back into the house. I then go inside and pick the phone up off of the floor. While putting the phone back together Paul begins cursing at me. My children still sitting on the porch and becoming more devastated seeing me going through another one of their future stepfather's rage.

Paul being furious walks up to me. "I should go get some gasoline and set your ass on fire!"

Thinking that he is just saying something to intimidate or put more fear in me, he then goes outside and gets the gas can from the back of the house. Coming back he asks his nephew to take him to the store. Minutes later they return.

As my children and I are still sitting here on the porch, Paul walked up to me and then pours some of the gas down on the grass where my feet are dangling, then takes a match and lights it, and throws it on the gas. As I am getting up off of the porch to keep myself from getting burned, Paul begins walking closer towards me again. In fear for my children, my nephew and Paul's nephew begin yelling at me to run.

As I take off running, Paul charges behind me with the container of gasoline. The faster I am running it seems to me the bigger the yard is getting. Thinking about it, . . . the yard is as big as a football field. I have almost ran this whole yard over and over again – zig zagging all over the place trying to get away from this madman. I am so tired, I just can't run anymore. In order to catch my breath I stopped running. My children and nephew then go into a panic stage.

They're yelling, "Please – please, . . . don't stop!"

"But I just can't run anymore!"

Paul catching up, now has gotten very close to me within dousing distance.

I said to him, "I am not running anymore! (still catching my breath) You just have to throw the gas on me. But if you do . . . and while I am burning . . . I am going to run you down grab a hold of you and we are both going to burn together!"

As he gets closer and not trusting him I take off running again. Finally, making it back to the porch Paul still cursing at me saying to me what he is going do to me. Walking up to me again he pours more gas down beside me. Hurrying to move I slid off the porch. While walking over to me Paul's nephew comes and grabs him by the arm, walks him over to the car, and makes him get inside.

While getting in the car Paul looks at me through the window and says to me, "Don't go to sleep!" They then pull out of the yard.

So tired and scared, I cannot move off of this porch; mentally frozen and unsure of anything. My children had to help me get inside. Once I snapped out of this horrible ordeal, I then looked at my children and requested that they make themselves some snacks while I go and get into the shower. Not knowing if Paul is going to turn around and come back, I hurried and got out of the shower. When finishing, I had the boys take a bath together to make it quick so my daughter can get in and out too.

After we all had our shower, I had them go into their bedrooms and get some blankets so we all can sleep in the living room. Being afraid I told them to go ahead and get some rest while I will keep watch over them. It has gotten later over into the night, but there is no sign of Paul in sight, but I am not trusting him. I then call one of my girlfriends telling her what had happened.

She said to me, "Girl, you need to get yourself some rest. It's going to be okay."

I said to her, "I really don't think I can, because sometimes when Paul says he is going to do something, he generally follows through with it. Look, I am very afraid he might come back and set the house on fire while the kids and I are asleep."

Hanging up the phone with her I then called the police.

One hour later as I am sitting here watching television and hearing a car passing, I get up go and look out of the window only to see it is the police passing. The thought comes into mind, we are so far away from the highway and it is so dark out here, we're in an area that I think we cannot ever be found.

The children are still asleep and I cannot leave them in the house alone to go and signal for the police to stop. I am now up walking the floors making sure Paul does not sneak back into the yard.

For me this is going to be a long night.

Chapter 23

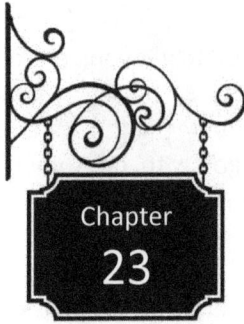

The following morning, the children are up early but I am still tired from the night before. After taking a shower and having breakfast the children wanting to go out to play, and because I need me some sleep I allowed them to go outside. I then go into my bedroom and get into my bed for a few hours. Upon waking up the children are now asking to walk to the store which is one mile away. While on our little walk the children begin laughing and talking about what happened on yesterday, my son and nephew saying we all wanted to jump on Paul and beat him down. To ease their minds and to reassure them that I am going to be okay, they all then gave a big sigh.

We are now on our way back home and out of nowhere my nephew asked, "Auntie, what will you do if Paul is at the house waiting on you with more gas?"

Laughing it off, "If he is there, I want you guys to stay away from him . . . and please don't say nothing either."

After getting to the house I open the door but there is no Paul. So I had the children straighten up their rooms while I put away the bags.

It is now late in the afternoon, Paul's nephew stopping by on his way from work to find out rather or not he came home from last night.

After telling him no, he says, "I took uncle Paul home with me thinking that he was going to spend the night, but he got out of the car and left walking up the street from my house," he continues, 'When I woke up and thinking maybe Uncle Paul was in bed . . . he wasn't. I'm sorry, but I really don't know where he could have spent the night."

I said to him, "I think it was best that he didn't come home."

Again, he apologizes for taking Paul to the store to get the gasoline.

While the children and I sit down to have dinner I explain to them, "If Paul comes home with more foolishness, you are not to get involved into the argument or fight but stay clear of Paul because I don't want you guys to get hurt. But, . . . I want you run as fast as you can up the street and get me some help, understand me?"

It is time to get settled in for the night. The kids go into the bedroom and I crashed on the couch.

Two days later Paul finally comes home. After getting up early and getting dressed there's a knock at the door. Thinking it is the landlord's husband I go and open the door. Upon opening the door Paul walks right pass me and goes into the bedroom, gets him some clothing and goes into the bathroom. He was in and out in a hurry. Getting out of the shower he goes back into the bedroom and gets into bed. I really don't know what his angle is this time, but I'm gonna keep an eye out for another one of his relentless fits he seems to have towards me and my children.

Coming into the living room where I am sitting I remind the children of our talk we had yesterday. They all are just sitting here looking in my face as if to say *and you think we paid you any attention*. As the time passes by very quickly it is already the afternoon. To get out of the house the children and I take a short walk up the street. Still tired from the night before we turn around and head back home. Going in through the backdoor Paul is now sitting in the living room watching television. In order not to be in his way my children and I decide to stay in the kitchen and play a few games.

While playing, they are constantly calling my name, "Mom . . . Mom . . . Mom," and asking me questions.

All of a sudden Paul yells into the kitchen, "If I hear any of you says *mom* one more time, I am going to throw something in there and hit you in the mouth!"

My nephew then yells out, "Mom," and begins laughing – giving Paul a smirky look.

I looked at Paul, then I looked at my nephew and said, "You better not bother him."

Paul gets up out of his chair and then walks out on the front porch.

After leaving out of the house the children go down the hallway saying to each other, "Why he didn't throw something like he said he was?"

Telling them to leave that alone they go into their rooms.

Minutes later, Paul returns back inside and goes back into the bedroom. I then called the children out of their rooms to have dinner trying to figure out why everyone is so quiet. I did everything I knew how to get them to talk (trying to make a conversation), but they didn't say a word. So, after dinner and excusing myself from the table I went into my bedroom.

Paul looking at me asked, "When is your nephew going home?"

Looking at him I asked in reply, "Why?"

He then says to me, "Because I am sick of his smart-ass mouth!"

I Looked at him and said, "Oh well," and walked out of the room. The children finish their dinner and goes back into their room, and we all called it a night.

One day later I am thinking that maybe things will get a little better if Paul and I get some relaxation time. So before leaving for work I decided to ask him that when he comes home, and if he would like to, we can take the children to my mother's house so we could go out together and shoot a few games of pool. He nodded and told me that this idea sounds like a winner.

After waking the children up, I asked them to pack an overnight bag because I made plans for them to stay at grandmas for tonight – and because Paul and I have plans. They hurried through their chores, pack their bags, and are now ready to leave.

5:00pm rolls around and Paul comes home from work. "Are the children ready to leave?"

After saying yes, he then takes a shower, gets dressed and then we all leave the house to take the children to my mother's.

Upon pulling into the driveway to leave the children with my mother, one of my brother's is coming to the car asking, "Where are you guys going?"

We both responded that we're going to the club to shoot a few games of pool.

Paul then asks him, "Would you like to join us?"

"Yes, I'm in." My brother then gets into the car with us.

After making it to the club and getting inside, we then find an available table start playing a few rounds of pool. Thinking about my children I get out of the game because I wanted to go and make sure they are okay. Paul and I leave the club to go check on my children. Getting to my mother's we both go inside. After talking with my mother for a little while, Paul says that we need to go back and get our table.

Upon returning to the club and thinking that I have gotten the keys out of the ignition, I locked the door by accident. We then go back inside and shoots a few more games. By now the club is getting crowded and it's to the point you can hardly move around. By this time it must be getting very late; according to how the club is picking up. I'm now ready to leave.

Paul and I left the club, but as we finally get to the car I begin searching my purse for the keys but they're not here. Not wanting to tell Paul about the keys being on the inside of the car, I continued to search my purse. Paul looking in the car at the ignition – and would you look at that, there they are . . . the keys. And of course we all knew what's coming next; as sure as a day of rain without an umbrella – and so is Paul's temper.

He begins yelling and cursing me out!

Trying so hard to explain to him I thought I had the keys, he just told me that he doesn't want to hear it. As I am still trying to explain he begins pushing me around. One of the guys that is standing near go back into the club and gets my brother. All of a sudden my brother walks around the corner and comes to me asking, "What is the problem?"

"I accidently locked the keys in the car."

Paul turns around and begins cursing at my brother. Standing here trying to talk with Paul he begins pushing me again. My brother then walks over to Paul and said, "Do not put your hands on her again!"

They begin to scuffle.

Knowing how my brother's temper is and not wanting things to get out of control, I then get in the middle of the two of them so that my brother will not get into any trouble over this man. Upon begging my brother to stop he then gets mad at me because I will not allow him to fight Paul.

"You are my sister and I don't like the fact you are letting this man push you around!"

I then go back inside of the club to get someone to assist us in getting the keys out of the car. After opening the door, Paul and I leave to go back by my mother's to once again check on my children before leaving to go home. Upon getting to my mother's house my children are now ready to leave with us. After getting their things we left to go home. While on our way home Paul tried to start to another argument in front of the children. Out of anger

I said to him that I am not going through this with him again, and that at this point – this conversation is over. Giving me a crazy look he lays his head against the window and falls asleep.

After getting home my children and I get out of the car and go inside of the house leaving Paul asleep in the car. Minutes later, Paul comes into the house and goes into the bedroom. Following him into the room he says to me, "Why did you leave me in the car asleep when you could have woke me up?"

Trying to be nice I said, "You were sleeping so well, and I had a feeling you didn't want to be bothered." Not knowing what's going through his mind, Paul walks up behind me and begin rubbing me on my shoulders. Softly shoving him away from me, he then goes into the living room – lays on the couch and fell back asleep.

I then pull off my clothes and get into bed . . . alone.

The following day, Paul and I get an early start because he has a job to go do and I have some errands to go run. After having breakfast my children and I leave to go visit my mother.

Getting to the house and as I walk inside, my brother coming up to me saying, "Whenever you and Paul gets into it again I am not getting in the middle, . . . only because I tried to defend you and you wouldn't even let me handled him."

Saying to him, "The reason I would not let you do it was because Paul was drunk and I knew you would have hurt him." He then just looks me in my face and walks away.

My mother wanting to know what happened on last night. Saying to her that the two of them, Paul and my brother were about to fight because I locked the keys in the car. She says to me that she would have let them fight. Looking at my mother, I just couldn't find it in my heart to let them fight. Not trying to let this conversation get out of hand, I left to go on my errands. One hour later I returned to my mother's and picked up my children and headed home.

After pulling into the back of the driveway Paul was

already there standing in the doorway. We got out of the car and went inside, my children headed to their bedrooms while I go into the living room to sit on the couch. Paul joining me in the living room comes and sits next to me. While talking to him I begin to tell him that my brother is very upset about what happened on last night. At this point he is pretending that he cannot remember any of it. I told myself that I better then just to leave the conversation alone altogether.

He then says to me that he made dinner, and that he wants me to call my children out of their rooms to eat. After fixing their plates I called them to the table. While eating no one is saying a word to each other. After finishing I went into my bedroom, grab our night things and prepare to get into the shower. Paul then comes into the bathroom asking, "Can I join you?" After telling him that I really don't want him to, he joins me anyway. After getting out of the shower we call it a night.

Chapter
24

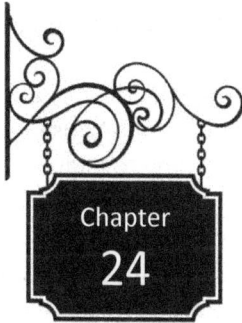

We're in the month of August and it is my brother's birthday. After getting out of bed I received a call asking if we will be coming to my mother's this afternoon to attend a cookout that's being held for my brother. Giving Paul the news he just says to me that he'll have things straightened out by the time I get home from work, he then leaves out of the house. Then I went and woke up my children and told them to clean the house and their bedrooms before you-know-who returns. Two hours later we are finished with the cleaning. Making a suggestion to my children that before Paul gets home from work, for the two of them to go ahead and get dress.

It is now 6:00pm. Paul returns home from work. By my children already being dressed, he and I then get dressed ourselves so we can leave to go to my mother's. I am really hoping that this turns out to be a good afternoon. Upon getting to my mother's there is already a crowd in the backyard. We all go around back, but for whatever reason my mother and her boyfriend gets into an argument. Thinking that I am going to get into the middle of it Paul says to me, "I hope you don't get upset and start nothing."

Looking him in his face I said to him, "Wait a minute, this is my mother and you are telling me not to say nothing? . . . What is wrong with you?" To put an end to the argument we all get my mother to calm down.

While we all are talking, all of a sudden my mother's boyfriend burst into tears and runs inside of the house. I followed him inside saying to him, "We are not going to allow you to talk to our mother the way you did." But I know that my mother is a strong enough woman to take control of any situation. So I then invites him back outside with me to have a little fun. Everyone is having such a good time but it has gotten really late and I am ready to go home. Paul requesting that I leave the children at my mother's for tonight, asking them if they like to stay the night. They both hurried and said yes. Paul and I then leave to go home. Seems to me it only took a few minutes and we were already pulling in the driveway.

After getting inside Paul goes in the bathroom and starts the shower. As I pull my shoes off he tells me to go ahead and get in. While I'm showering he lets out the sofa bed. After I was done, I'm ready for bed. Paul walks up behind me and says that tonight we are sleeping in the living room. While he gets into the shower I go ahead and get relaxed. Minutes later Paul comes and lays next to me, he then tells to me this is how it should be.

I asked him, "What are you talking about?"

He says to me, "Just the two of us." He then looks at me and says, "I want to make love to you."

Saying to myself, "I know you are not saying this to me after what just came out of your mouth."

But in order for this not to turn into an argument or a fight, I give in and make love with him.

While falling asleep Paul turns to me and holds me in his arms saying to me, "This is it . . . no children."

Sick and tired of him saying this, I then get up and go into the bathroom. Standing in front of the mirror saying to myself that it will never happen; I am not getting rid of my children for him. I then left out of the bathroom went back into the living room and laid behind Paul and fell asleep.

#####

Two weeks later Paul and I get up early this morning because we are having a big cookout for my son, his uncle, nephew and himself. Having to go to the grocery store to buy the food to prepare for the event I had my children to go ahead and get dressed. After returning to get things started my children and I cleaned the house while Paul cleans the yard and cuts the grass. After minutes of cleaning the house I then get started on cleaning the meats to be put on the grill. About a half hour later some of Paul friends arrives at the house, Paul stopping with the grass invites them to come inside, then he went outside to wash off the grill to start the meat.

Seconds later after starting the grill my son and my nephew decides to go outside and shoot a few games of basketball, I let them know that it was okay. While preparing some of the other foods, I begin hearing Paul on the outside, shouting and screaming to the top of his lungs at the boys.

"Why are you guys playing basketball while I am cooking on the grill?! . . . And I know you see the dust flying in the air!"

Rushing outside to find out what is the problem.

Paul cursing and yelling.

I said to him, "Paul, how is it possible when the basketball hoop is so far away from the grill, and there is no dust flinging near you?"

Still cursing. "I do not give a dam how far it may be . . . make them put the basketball away!"

Not wanting this to blow up in front of company I ask the boys to please put the ball down.

My son then asked, "Why are you scared of that man?" He and my nephew then headed back inside of the house and went into his bedroom.

As I was near the window, I heard one of the men talking to Paul. "Let me tell you something, the boys really wasn't making any dust, but are you forgetting that her son is getting bigger and he is going to remember how you are treating him, . . . and then is going to whip your behind."

After hearing Paul laughing it off, I then move away from the window.

It's now 5:00pm, people are beginning to arrive and they are going around to the back of the house, Paul then comes inside and gets into the shower. While he's doing so, I go outside and greet the guests. Everyone was having a good time until my brother and his girlfriend arrives. And for whatever reason, they are beginning to open beer after beer, and sitting them on the ground. Rather Paul saying something to the both of them, he starts an argument with only my brother. My brother then gets upset with his girlfriend and begins to argue with her. Having to calm them down for at least a moment they go their separate ways.

It is now beginning to get dark and we all go inside. At this point, all of the food is gone but there are a few people that are still hungry, so we decided to go get Chinese carry out. On my way to pick up the food, I said to Paul, "Make sure you keep everything under control until I return."

Well that did not happen, after returning and getting inside all of the children are now in a room together. I go down the hall to find out why are they in there. All of a sudden everyone begins to run to the front door. I then leave out of the room to see my brother and his girlfriend in the backyard fighting. When I questioned Paul about what happened after I left the house, he just looked at me with no response but only downing his head. So I then go back into the room where the children are, and they all begin to telling their side of the story; which was pretty much the same.

"While you were gone your brother was outside with the

others, and his girlfriend was in here standing in front of the television while Paul was sitting in the chair watching."

"Watching what?"

"She began to dance crazy-like, . . . and while dancing she begin to pull off her clothes. Paul then rushed us out of the room."

"Then what happened?"

"Well, afterwards your brother came in and pushed her to the floor . . . yep. That's when Paul got up out of his chair and pushed your brother out of the front door."

I then go back into the living room again and asked Paul, "What happened when I left here?"

He is still not saying a word, and my brother's girlfriend sitting in the corner looking acting like if she's lost. Upset I ask her to leave out of my house and my yard.

"Girl, . . . not only did you disrespected my home but also my children. You gotta go! . . . Get the rest of your clothes up off the floor and get the hell out of my house now!"

Paul gets upset with me and begins at cursing me in front of everyone that is left in the house. Trying so hard to hold it together because I am refusing to argue in front of all these people, out of the blue someone makes a comment saying to Paul, "I don't mean any harm but you are looking very bad (poking his finger into Paul's chest), as if you are being mistreated . . . and you need to leave her alone."

Now that struck my last nerve! My mouth is now about to move – letting everyone know what the hell is really going on. But before I got the chance to say anything, Paul stood up looks at me, then at everyone and said to them, "The reason why I look the way I do is because I've been out of work and I haven't been feeling well."

Looking at the person that's doing the talking I said to myself, "How come you think he is the one being mistreated? If only you knew the hell me and my children are going through."

Everyone now decides to leave, it turned out so wrong with all this backdrop commotion. So I go into the kitchen and begin to clean up the mess. Paul seeing everyone out and saying his goodnights – like he's not feeling it too.

He then comes into the kitchen asking, "Are you upset about the comment that was made?"

In response I said to him, "Why are you hiding and not telling these people your real problem? And one more thing, . . . anytime you feel like leaving (expressing it sternly) you are always welcome to go!"

He just walks away.

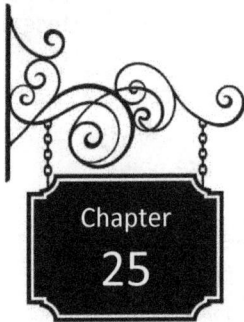

Chapter
25

The following day trying to get some sleep Paul gets up very early because his uncle stayed overnight. He's up yelling for coffee, so we all just get out of bed. Hearing Paul saying to his uncle that he hated the fact that he cannot see his children, I then walk into the living room pretending that I hadn't heard what was said. Being cautious this morning, I quietly walk over to the chair and sit down and look at the two of them having their own conversation without joining in. Seconds later the telephone rings. When I answered, someone was calling for Paul stating that he had a job for him to do. After hanging up the phone and informing him, he says to me that he is going to it and that he will have to leave, and that he need for me to keep his uncle company.

After Paul leaves the house, a few minutes later his uncle is asking me questions.

"Do you love my nephew?"

"Yes."

He looks me in my eyes and ask, "Why?"

I thought about it for a second, then said, "In some ways Paul can be a nice person at times, but when it comes to other people he can laugh and have a good time. But to me, he acts as if it is a hard thing to do with me." Who am I fooling . . . giving it some thought, I decided to tell him the truth.

It seemed like that is what he was expecting to hear, . . . the truth.

His uncle then says to me, "I can tell by the way you act. And I know Paul have been abusing you and those children." Being very concerned he continues, "Why don't you just leave him, I am just hoping that you don't let him hurt you or the children."

Thinking about what Paul said to his uncle earlier I picked up the telephone goes into the bedroom. I then call one of his family members to get a number to contact his children. While on the telephone I begin to hear Paul's uncle asking my children a similar question, "How does the two of you feel about Paul?"

My daughter responded, "I am alright with him as long as he don't hit me."

My son immediately expressed how he felt, "I don't like the man!"

I guess that is all his uncle needed to hear. After that, the house was quiet and we felt relaxed for a change.

A few hours later Paul returns home, but I am waiting until he gets comfortable before I tell him that I have a number for him to get in contact with his children.

As I begin dinner I am thinking of a way to break it to him. While preparing the meal, Paul comes into the kitchen to offer me a hand. So, at that moment I decided to seize the opportunity – I handed him the number.

Looking very surprised he asks, "What is this?"

I said, "Just call your children."

He gets upset and begin yelling, "How did you get the number?!"

"Well I got the number from your mother-in-law."

"Who the hell are you to go behind my back and call that woman?!"

"Because I heard you said to your uncle that you are here with my children and you cannot talk with your own." You can just about feel the tension brewing up. "Now that you have the number you can go ahead and call them."

I then quickly walked away from him as he is still holding that piece of paper in his hand with the number on it.

While dinner is cooking my children and I go outside to play a few games of basketball, my son saying to me, "Mom, why did you do that for him when you know he was going to curse you out?"

Saying to him in response, "Because I am tired of his mouth."

After playing a few games of ball we decided to walk to my girlfriend's house which is two miles away. When we arrived, it was only to find out that she wasn't home. So we begun to turn around and head back home. Getting back to our place, I set the table so that my children and I can have a nice dinner together. While eating dinner Paul seems much calmer. I suppose he thought about it a little; in knowing that I was only trying to help. He looked up at me from across the room and gets up out of his chair – walking over to me and begins apologizing for the way he acted earlier.

I said to him, "I only did what I thought was right for you."

As he walks away he says to me, "I really appreciate what you have done. All I ever wanted to know is what's going on with them." As he tries to show a little compassion he continues, "Also, while you guys were out I called their mother and she informed me they will be arriving in a few days to visit."

Since I opened this door, at this point all I can say is that sounds good to hear. Hoping this makes a big difference, especially from the way things are now going. After getting out of the shower we all called it a night.

A few days later, I received a telephone call requesting that I appear for work. After getting dressed we all leave the house. Only having a few hours to work I am thinking 'should I go home or go to my mother's house.' With the time passing by so fast my work day is now over. I ended up walking to my mother's to see if all is well with her. Upon getting there and realizing that I will be needing a ride home later on, I then pick up the telephone and calls Paul to let him know I am at my mother's house.

One hour later Paul arrives to pick me up. On our way home he decides to go by his mother's house first. As we get close to her house Paul noticed that she is standing in the front yard with two other people, he then passes on through without stopping. He then says to me, "I wonder who they were she was standing with running her mouth?" I just kept quiet, not wanting to comment on anything. Home was too close to even think about getting into a mix with Paul.

After getting home I get out of the truck, go inside put my things away, and begin to get ready for my children to return from school. I laid on the couch for only just a moment, but apparently I must of fallen asleep because I am being awakened by noises coming from my children and Paul. While speaking with Paul the telephone rings, I then answer it only to hear that it is Paul's mother asking to speak with him. Before giving Paul the phone she says to me, "I seen when the two of you passed my house. I didn't know if you were with him or not, but his wife and daughter are here and I didn't want to stop him because I didn't know how you would have taken it."

After hearing her speak I say to her, "I would have been okay with it because I will not keep him away from his children."

She continues on to talk as if she's trying to upset me, so I hurried and passed the phone to Paul; really not wanting to hear what she is saying to him. But whatever it may be, he's only saying great.

While Paul goes into the bedroom my children and I go ahead and have dinner. Having the chance to enjoy our little dinner, we laughed and talked about anything they wish to talk about. It really felt good for a change!

After finishing our dinner, they went into their bedrooms and got prepared for the following day while I clear the table. Paul then comes out of the bedroom asking me, "Do you have to go to work in the morning?"

Letting him know that I am not sure, I then in turn asked him, "Why are you asking?"

He gives no answer in return.

I then go and get my night things and gets into the shower.

Upon returning back into the bedroom at this point Paul is pretending to be asleep, so I get into bed and turn my back to him.

Two days later Paul leaves early for work without saying a word to anyone. After my children leave for school and knowing that I need the rest I go and get back into bed. Suddenly being awakened by a noise in the kitchen I jump out of bed and tiptoe to the kitchen door to see who it may be in the house, but it's only Paul fixing himself some lunch. As I step in Paul says to me that he will be getting off from work early so he can go spend some time with his daughter. All I can say is that it's fine with me, and that should make him feel much better.

It is now 4:00pm, Paul and my children arrived home at the same time.

Paul being excited and nervous at the same time said to me, "You and your children need to be ready to leave by the time I freshen up, because I am going to drop you guys at your mother's while I go get my daughter." Minutes later we were ready to leave.

The moment had finally came for Paul's reunion with his daughter. He dropped us off at my mother's and he then left to go pick up his daughter. As I walk into my mother's house she looked at me asking why were we here.

"Mom, Paul's daughter is in town visiting her grandmother, and he's going to pick her up so he can spend time with her. He's probably going to be bringing her by for a little while."

We all are just sitting around patiently waiting for their return when my mother asks, "Will she be staying at your home?"

I didn't know what to tell her, all I can say is, "From the way he has been acting, I really don't think that would be a good idea."

While we're talking, Paul pulls into the driveway and they both get out of the car. As I go outside to greet her, Paul introduced me to her as his friend. Never saying hello, she's just standing here looking at me with a strange look on her face. He then grabs her by the hand and says, "Here, let's go inside so you can meet the rest of these people." Knowing he's speaking of my children and the rest of my family.

As she is being introduce to the rest of the family, she is standing here with her little nose turned up. She then looks at him and says, "I am ready to leave." They then left out of the house.

Following behind the two of them, Paul says to me, "I am taking her to see my uncle that lives down the street."

Asking him, "Would you like for me to walk with you guys?"

Paul saying to me, "You can come if you want too . . . or you can stay here, the choice is yours."

So I made it my choice to go.

While walking down the street – they both walking ahead of me, I overheard him say to her, "This is what we call the country, and so are the people here."

Saying to myself, "I know he is not calling me and my family country," but I am just going to keep my mouth shut.

Spending a little time with the uncle down the street, Paul is now ready to leave to go visit another uncle. At this point he says to me, "You can stay here, and if I am not back by the time you guys are ready to leave, you can go ahead and find you a ride home."

My children looked at me and said, "Mom, you are so stupid! He acted like you were a *no-body*."

In shock, I said to them, "I do not want to hear you guys say that ever again!"

It is now 8:00pm, and my children and I having to walk to the store to find a ride home. Luckily, by seeing the old man who is always riding people around, this would be our ticket back home. So I walked up to him and I kindly asked if he could take me and my children home.

"Sure, . . . get in. You and your children shouldn't be out here this time of night looking for a ride home." He goes on to say, "that man of yours should be ashamed of himself, anything can happen to you and those children."

Upon getting home, my children and I go inside to get settled down. While they are getting prepared for the following day I make a snack for the three of us; having a thought that there is a possibility Paul may not be coming home tonight. It is now six hours later and Paul finally returns home. The problem is he's not saying much about the time he spent with his daughter – he's only talking about his wife.

Here it is, I have no clue what happened between the two of them, but whatever it is he's very upset about the visit. Therefore, I am not going to ask him to talk about it because knowing him he's only going to curse me out. Paul then gets up out of his chair looks out of the front door and goes into our bedroom.

While watching television I call my children out of their bedrooms to spend some time with me. As we're sitting here and with my son just looking at me shaking his head, before he can say anything I said to him "Do not say nothing to get Paul started, because we all know he don't want me talking to you guys, . . . but you guys are my children."

All of a sudden Paul comes out of the living room and goes into the bathroom – hearing him talking to himself. Thinking that he is talking about my children, they excuse themselves and went back into their bedrooms leaving me sitting here alone. Waiting until Paul finishes in the bathroom, I then go into our bedroom and get my night things so I can get in the shower myself.

Upon him coming out and me going in, he's still talking to himself. And for whatever reason, he goes through the house turning out all of the lights. I hurried up and got out of the shower and go back into the bedroom and get in bed. Here comes Paul into the room with something seriously on his mind, but we're not saying anything to each other. At this moment, it's good to keep that way for now. This time getting in bed, he turns his back on me and goes to sleep.

Chapter
26

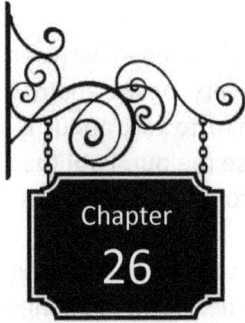

Weeks later, upon picking up the mail this morning there's a letter stating that Paul has to go back to court for child support. I am a little worried, but I won't let it get the best of me. While on his break, Paul makes a stop by the house for lunch. After receiving all the mail, he opens the letter finding he only have a short period of time before appearing in front of the judge. Knowing we don't have enough money to obtain a lawyer, Paul looks at me and says, "Why are you so worried? I have everything under control." He then leaves and goes back to work.

Needing some time for myself I leave the house to go visit my mother. Upon getting to her house only to see she's not home. I then decide to take a walk to the store. While on my way, I run into this guy that's always walking and talking to himself. As I get close to him, I say to him, "I am so glad to see you." Explaining to him the problems that Paul is having with the court system. He explains to me his situation, saying that the best thing for him to do is go visit the V.A. Hospital to get some help. Upon walking away, I am trying to figure out how we're going to do this when I; speaking of myself, don't even have a car anymore.

After getting what I needed from the store, instead of going back to my mother's I decide to catch a ride and go home. Standing here hoping someone comes through, I didn't feel like sticking around, so I left and started walking. Just my luck Paul saw me and pulls into the parking lot.

"How did you get here?"

"I walked to the main highway and caught someone to my mother's house."

"But you were supposed to be at home. Get in here and let me take you home."

On our way back home we are not saying a word to each other; just total and utter silence.

After getting home I make a few telephone calls to make arrangements to get Paul an appointment at the V.A. Hospital. Being that he has gotten accepted to see a doctor, I went ahead and begin dinner for tonight.

Minutes later, my children arrives home from school. While getting undressed I make their plates to eat. I already know when Paul gets here he's going to be upset as usual, I also know that they don't need to hear anything of what he has to say.

It's 5:00pm, Paul walks through the door and my children excuses themselves and goes directly into their bedrooms like clockwork. Paul and I then go into the living room. While he is talking about his day, I gently break it to him that I made some calls and have set and appointment with the V.A. Hospital. Paul looking frustrated at me saying, "There you go again, always going behind my back and doing things without talking it over with me. I hope you know what you are doing." He then gets up and goes into the bedroom. So here we are again, another night going to bed without nothing to say to each other. At this point it's not bothering me anymore. We haven't even touched each other for some time now anyway.

The following day the children are at school and Paul is at work. I am just sitting here in these woods with all kinds of thoughts going through my mind. For whatever reason, I come with the ideal notion of Paul taking a few days off from work until he gets this child-support under control. 12:00pm, Paul comes home for lunch. While sitting at the dinner table and bringing up my idea, shockingly Paul saying to me that he is going to go along with it only for a little while, but we will finish discussing this matter when he returns home this evening. He then leaves the house.

3:00pm came, and my children are now at home. As they walk through the door, they both asked the question, "Where is Paul?"

Saying to them, "He's at work."

Replying with a smart remark, "Oh, we thought he would be in jail."

Looking at the two of them. "You guys know that you're both wrong for saying that."

They just roll their eyes at me and went into their rooms and began their normal chores.

While making dinner my children decides to go for a walk before Paul returns home from work. When they asked me, I told them that it was okay, but just a short one. I then make a few more phone calls to get the help I need in order to properly help Paul. Time going so fast again that 7:00pm was without a moment's notice. My children and Paul has already returned home. Well then, I guess we all sit down and have dinner.

While eating, I then bring up the subject again. Paul looking at me and slammed his fork on the table and ask, "How in the hell are these bills going to get paid?"

Waiting for a second, I said to him, "Listen, either you need my help or not. I have already planned to get a second job. But it can be done differently if you wish for it to happen."

Paul just looks at me and says, "I hope this works," then picked up his fork and continued eating.

My children gets up from the table and leaves out of the kitchen. I could only try to imagine what they are thinking of me right about now. But it's so hard to explain things to them that I am only helping Paul because I had made him a promise – and within that promise, in hoping that he will get better. I then excused myself and left to take a shower because I really need to clear my head. I am wondering what is wrong with me. After my shower, I go into my bedroom and calls it a night.

Weeks have now passed. Paul is still not working and it is really getting harder on me, which I thought was going to be easy. I am only making enough money just to make the ends meet. Knowing that I can't make it happen. I turned to my mother for help, but she can only tell me that she can only give me what she has. She then goes on to say that she is only doing this because of my children, and most of all, why is she doing this anyway. Explaining to her a little more in detail, I then pleaded with her to never tell Paul that I came by asking her for help. She then reminded me that she doesn't mind because I'm her daughter, and that's what mother's do for their children. After I gave her a hug and a kiss, I then left to go pay part of the bills.

Tired from all the walking I tried to find a ride home. I am hoping by the time I get there, Paul will have dinner cooked. Finally, I makes it home! But, there's no dinner and Paul is high as a kite. I'm just wondering, with having not working and no money, how is he always able to get high? Let alone, make it home to eat? Anyway, with tears in my eyes I put my things down and go into the bedroom. While lying down for a while, I apparently must have I fallen quickly asleep again, because when I heard my children coming into the house I jumped out of bed. I then stretched my arms and yawned a little, and headed into the living room to go greet them home.

When I approached them with open arms, my son just looked at me in disappointment and said, "This is what you want to come home to everyday," he then shakes his head and grabs his school stuff and goes into his bedroom.

Not wanting to cook – but I have no choice because at this point Paul is not capable of turning on the stove. Giving myself a few minutes to calm my nerves and knowing my children and I have to eat, I then go ahead and make dinner. A few hours later dinner is ready, and as usual my children and I sat down to eat together. While eating, my children and I are talking about how their day went. Glancing into the living room to notice Paul just sitting there staring into our faces like he has something to say, considering being high and all. So I continued to talk with my children as if he wasn't there.

Upon finishing our meal my children goes into their rooms. As I get into the living room I begin to talk with Paul about my day. Never mentioning that I visited my mother, he is just sitting there glassy-eyed with that nasty candy cane aroma acting like I haven't said a word.

Saying to myself, "I am not going to bother to ask about his day, because I already seen how it went. But I am still trying to figure out how is it that you are here all day with no money, and yet you are high."

Knowing my children needs some time away from this I go into their rooms tells them to pack some things because I am allowing them to go spend some time with my mother they seem not to waste any time getting packed. After talking with them I go get into the shower and calls it a night because at this point I just can't stand seeing Paul.

The following day I am really getting tired of this, I have to go to work and Paul stays at home. My day at work is going to be longer than I thought and how far it would be to walk, but at least I will have peace of mind. The day finally ended and I'm on my way home from work. After leaving the job, I decided go to my mother's house and wait on my children to get here. Now here and while waiting, my mother asked, "How are you going to make it like this, . . . you're working and he is just sitting on his ass?" I really can't come out and tell her it was planned this way, all I can say to her is that I can manage it.

Thirty minutes later my children arrives; they are so happy to be here with my mother. My daughter asking, "Are you staying here too?"

Saying to her, "No, I have to go home . . . but I will see you guys on tomorrow."

After giving them a hug and a kiss I get my things together and leave to go home. After getting home I go inside to find this is day two, he is high and still no food cooked.

"What is your excuse you didn't cook today?"

He says to me, "Because you didn't tell me what you wanted to eat."

In response I say to him, "I really didn't figure that I had to make a menu."

He then gets mad and walks out of the front door.

Hurrying to the window to see if he is hanging out in the yard. Instead, he's walking towards the highway. Feeling kind of bad and tired I go and make me something quick to eat.

Noticing it is now beginning to get dark outside and Paul haven't returned, I am thinking that maybe he walked to the main highway to catch a ride to our hometown. Thinking to myself and realizing that I am out here in the middle of nowhere alone, I grab my purse to leave the house and begin walking to the main highway myself. It is so dark on this road you cannot see nothing, and I don't know what may come out and cross the road. As I am walking I begin talking to myself hoping this will help me get to the highway faster. Finally, I reach the main highway. So afraid to stop anyone for a ride, I decide to walk over to one of Paul's cousin house. And would you look at this, here he is standing near a fire with some other guys.

Walking over to him I asked, "Why did you leave the house without saying something to me?"

He begins to get loud – saying to me, "Who asked you to come over here?"

"You know what? . . . You're right!" I begin to walk off.

At this point, I don't know if I want to go home or go to my mother's. Scared out of my wit I begin to walk back towards home. I take off walking very fast, but seems to me it has gotten darker than before. When I reached this certain area, I begin hearing someone calling my name. Too scared to stop I continued to walk *just a little faster*. All of a sudden, I turn around to see it's Paul. As I reach this steep high hill which is only a block away from the house I stop to rest. Paul then caught up with me. He is so drunk, and by knowing he cannot make it up the hill alone – in my mind I am wanting to leave him here. Instead, I grab him by the hand and walked with him until we got to the top of the hill.

We are now only a few minutes away from the house, I then let go of his hand. Again he began stumbling. So I turned around and went back to help walk him home with me. After reaching the house and opening the door I helped him to the couch. Shaking my head, I lay him down. I then go into the bedroom and sit on the bed, asking myself why am I being such fool. Too angry to search inside of myself for the answer, too tired from all that walking, and basically dragging Paul home, I found my way into the shower to wash away all the stress.

Standing here just letting the hot water trickle down on me, all sorts of thoughts and flashbacks are going through my mind. I'm wanting to cry so badly, but the tears just won't fall. So I take my time to get out. After showering, I go into the living room to see if Paul is okay, only to find him fast asleep. I then go and get into bed. After falling asleep myself, I am being awakened by Paul getting into bed beside me. Not bothering to move, he's just lying here talking to himself. Now that I am awake, I am not going back to sleep until I know he's completely out. A few seconds later, he's now out cold snoring – now I know I can get me rest.

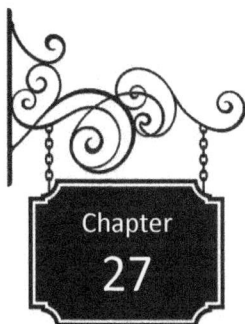

Chapter
27

It is now time for Paul to visit the V.A Hospital.

After seeing my children off to school Paul and I get dressed. Having to go to his mother's house to use her car, we begin walking to the main highway to catch a ride to get there. After walking about one mile or two we finally catch a ride. Upon making it to his mother's we get her car and headed to the V.A.

After getting to the hospital Paul asking, "What am I supposed to do?"

Saying to him, "I will help you."

We then go inside.

Sitting here for almost two hours, he is finally being seen by a doctor, but he is giving him such a hard time because he is saying that Paul reeks the smell of alcohol, and it will be a waste of his time. Looking into my man's face I asked him about the drinking. He says to me that he does not drink alcohol. Well, this is an unexpected answer!

Having to go see another doctor, at this point he's being told the reason he is having seizures is because it is caused by an alcohol withdrawal, and all he can do is just look at him.

On our way home we are not saying nothing to each other. The stillness we now have between ourselves is really sickening. Getting to his mother's house to return her car she began asking questions to what was said at the doctor's office. I feel since he's not saying nothing, then why should I volunteer.

As we get home we are still not saying a word to each other. I then prepare snacks for my children until they return home from school. While doing so, Paul goes into the bedroom. I then go outside and sit on the front porch and wait on the bus to arrive. Minutes later, my children are home. We go inside to have a snack together. Before anything got started, I told them to please do not ask Paul about how did things go because I really don't feel like arguing today – let this be one of our good ones. So we quietly had our snacks while talking about our day. When finished, they got up and went into their bedroom.

Now sitting here in the living room alone for which I am so tired of this; only spending a few minutes with my children because of this man not wanting them talking with me – I just feel trapped in a relation that is out of control. I then call one of my mother's neighbors. Listening to her talk about everything that had happened in the neighborhood, Paul walking out of the bedroom comes over to me wanting to know who I am talking with. Then he invites himself to sit next to me and interrupts my phone conversation asking, "Are you done yet?"

Saying to her, "Look, I'm sorry but I have to go."

She says to me, "Just give me a call when you can, . . . and I mean when you have time," she then hangs up on her side first.

While he's still sitting there next to me even after I hung up the phone staring and not saying a word, I guess I had nothing to say either. So I got up and ended my evening very early.

A few weeks later Paul finally returns to work. Now things change? He says to me, "I can't stand sitting around the house without enough money coming in. And I am tired of putting the responsibility on you because it is your job to take care of your children." But he is always saying to me that he is not going to spend any of his own money on them, . . . don't figure.

Upon everyone leaving for the day, I catches me a ride from one of our neighbors and go to my mother's house to spend some *mother and daughter time* together. Getting to my mother's we begin to have a great time – we laugh and talk about a little bit of everything and everybody. I really needed this time with her. It's getting late and now it's time to go home. At least we had a good time together.

As I am walking from my mother's I decide to visit the man that lives only a few houses from my mother. Sitting under the tree he says to me, "Come and have a seat with me."

Upon walking over and sitting next to him he asks, "Why do you have this look on your face as if you are worrying about something?"

Not being able to say a word the tears begin to flow down my face. I started telling him about the problems I am having in my life. He then looks me in my face and asked, "Do you love the boy?"

Saying to him, "You know what . . . at this point, I really do not know."

He goes on to say, "I can tell. But you cannot let anyone treat you wrong. And I know what's going on, I have been where you are heading. The hurt is very painful and it will leave a stain on you for the rest of your life, but all you have to do is trust in God and allow him to work this out for you and your children. Now I want you to go home and begin reading your bible from the beginning and to the end. You will get strong enough to do what is right. In the meantime, I am going to end this conversation until the next time." Looking at me with all sincerity he says, "Now get up and go home."

While walking to the store to catch a ride back home I begin to think, "What is the moral to the story?"

Arriving at the store, there is the old man sitting in the parking lot. So I walked over to him and asked if he can please give me another ride home again. He just says, "Girl, get in the car."

Riding down the highway he says to me, "I have nothing to do with your business, but listen to me very carefully girl. Why are you staying with this boy when he has you walking and trying to find rides home, . . . and knowing it is not a good thing (then he shrugs his shoulder). But, I'm just saying, he rides around in the company truck looking like he is high all day." As I am taking a mental note without saying a word he continues, "A lot of fellas have said they would be glad to help you and your children, but as long as you are with Paul they won't. And, they really feel sorry for you."

Still can't utter a word, all I can do is just hold my head down.

Finally making it home, I get out of the car and told the old man, "Thank you so much for the ride and the talk."

After getting inside I am wondering why are both of these men talking to me on the same subject. Minutes later my children comes into the house. When my son got inside, the first thing he asked is, "Where's Paul?"

Seems like nothing changed, so I responded nicely, "Why?"

Disrespectfully he says to me, "Because he is not sitting in his favorite chair popping tops (meaning beer cans)." He then laughs in my face and continues laughing as he goes down the hallway to his bedroom.

The telephone then rings. To my surprise it is my girlfriend from another state – implying that she will be coming for a visit to spend some time with me and my children. Before giving her an answer I informed her that I would have to talk it over with Paul, but I will return her call as soon as possible, and hoping that he will say yes.

After hanging up and not knowing Paul was already outside on the back porch during that time, I assume that he probably heard me on the phone. So just in case, I asked my children to sit still and don't say a word to Paul about my conversation with my girlfriend. They both look at me and said that they won't, just because hellraiser is out there and they would rather go to their bedrooms.

As they head down the hallway, Paul walks inside then goes into the bedroom rolls up him a joint, and then goes back out into the front yard, and sits under a tree.

While putting the dinner on the table, the telephone again rings – it is once again my girlfriend. At this point my children are sitting down having dinner. Feeling a little scared, I go ahead and walk out front and asked Paul the question. "Paul, will it be okay if my girlfriend come spend some time with us?"

He says to me, "Tell her she's welcome to do so."

Looking at him like, 'Wow! Who is this person? Paul must have gotten lost on the way home.'

After dinner while my children and I are sitting here watching television, my son says to me, "Mom you need to be careful because there could be a catch behind his answer." But I have already had that thought in mind.

Being so excited that my girlfriend will be visiting, I go ahead and end the night early.

YEAR

1 9 9 9

Chapter
28

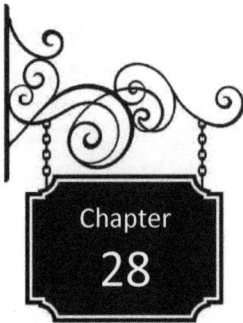

My girlfriend finally arrives!

Having to wake up early because I need to clean the house and go grocery shopping. So excited because it has been many years since I've seen her. After I had finished with my cleaning, it was now time to go run my errands while my children goes to my mother's house to spend time with her. After getting there and telling everyone the good news about my girlfriend's arrival in a few hours, they were all are very excited.

Time has now past and we have to leave to return home to get prepared. While on my way, I am thinking how I am going to get my girlfriend from the train station. So I had to make a stop by my sister-in-law's house and ask her to drive because I am not familiar with the area. Upon pulling into her driveway she meets me at the door. Explaining to her that I need her help she says to me, "It is not a problem . . . and I will be there."

When I got home, Paul was already there. Seems that he has already gotten off from work early. As I was coming in through the doorway he came over to me and said, "Have your children get settled in and I'll make dinner because you have been out and you are already running behind schedule, . . . and that you need to leave the house."

At this very moment while talking, my sister-in-law pulls

into the driveway. I grab my purse and walked out of the house. As we leave, I am hoping we get there on time.

My sister-in-law said to me, "You should be very excited because you have someone to be with you out in these woods."

"But I wonder how long Paul is planning to make her comfortable so that she can stay," I said in reply.

Once we arrived at the train station, she was already waiting for me. My girlfriend has been standing outside the station only for a little while. As my sister-in-law parks the car I jump out and run to her. We were so happy to see each other, tears began rolling down our faces. Upon leaving the train station, my girlfriend and I were catching up on old times and lost loves. Being that it is late, when we returned home everyone has already fell asleep. I then go down the hallway to wake up my children so that they can give my girlfriend the greeting that they have been anticipating on.

After the children gave their own special celebrated greeting, we all decided to stay up a little while longer. It was great! Talking and having so much fun, it was almost too good to be true. By the time our fun slowed down, it was almost morning.

Paul comes out of the bedroom asking me, "Are you planning to get any sleep?"

I Looked at him and said, "I'm sorry, I really didn't pay any attention to the time."

I excused myself, leaving my girlfriend and my children sitting in the living room I go and get into bed. While lying there, I hear my girlfriend asking my children, "Does your mother do everything he tells her to do?" While still listening, in return I heard the both of them tell her yes. But I was too tired to get out of bed and go back into the living room to put my two cents into it. So I just let it be for now and fell asleep.

The following day, not knowing why Paul got out of bed early but I decided to stay in bed a little while longer. All of a sudden, Paul's standing in the middle of the hallway yelling for everyone to get out of bed. Coming out of our bedrooms to see what all the yelling is about, Paul said to us, "You guys go into the kitchen because breakfast is on the table." We all then go wash up and head to the kitchen table.

While sitting at the table Paul says, "I have somewhere to go," he then leaves out of the house.

My girlfriend says to me, "Look hun, there's something about your man I do not like."

All I can do is just give her a smile.

It is the middle of the afternoon. Paul returns home, and to top it all off – in front of my company he is high. Here he comes strolling into the house looking at everyone in a strange way and then goes into the bedroom. To keep my girlfriend from noticing him I continue to talk, but she just gives me this look.

A few hours later my family now have arrived. Paul then comes out of the bedroom asking, "Have you offered anyone something to eat?" Everyone saying to him they have already eaten before leaving home. I then go ahead and fix my children and girlfriend something to eat while the rest of us sit around and talk.

It has now gotten late and everyone is beginning to leave to go home. I then begin cleaning the house while Paul and my girlfriend talk about her trip here. After finishing, Paul gets up and goes back into the bedroom. As I sit down to get me some rest, my girlfriend asked, "Where did you get him from?"

Saying to her, "Standing on a corner by a store."

She burst out laughing. "Well, you need to take him back!"

Not saying it out loud, but in my mind I wished I did.

After talking for a while I then get up and head into my bedroom and get my night things together. After that, I went in the bathroom to take my shower. Upon getting ready to turn the shower on, Paul comes in the bathroom to join me, asking, "How long will your friend be staying here?"

Wondering why is he asking me this, I responded carefully. "I am not sure, because she said to me it is only going to be for maybe about . . . two weeks, because she wants to spend some time with me and other family members, then she will be returning home."

He just looks at me and says okay. So after our shower together, we go back into the bedroom and say our goodnights.

Days have now passed and my girlfriend hasn't went to visit any of her other family members. Paul is now asking the same question, "When is she leaving here?" Being that she is my friend, I just can't find the way to go and ask her this. We both then decided to leave out of the house for awhile.

Having being out for a few hours I return home to find my girlfriend still sitting around in her night clothes, but the house is cleaned. After putting my things away my girlfriend is asking me to have a seat. While sitting here, she says to me that she's been making a few phone calls and that she will be giving me $99 dollars per month to help out with my household bills. Thinking to myself, *"How am I going to tell Paul that she will not be leaving anytime soon?"* and knowing how he is going to react to the news.

While beginning dinner, Paul and my children arrives home. My children began their chores while Paul goes straight to the bedroom. At this point I'm not going to bother Paul, but I do have to talk with him. My girlfriend and I decided to work together in the kitchen to make a few snacks for everyone. While making the snacks, I had to tell her that I have not spoken to Paul yet on the decision that she made to stay awhile longer.

Calling my children out of their rooms to the dinner table and still upset from what I said, my girlfriend in the meantime excuses herself and goes into the bedroom. Paul then comes out of our bedroom and goes outside to sit under the tree in the front yard and smoke a joint.

After we all finish our snacks we went outside also, but

to only sit on the porch. At this point, Paul are now high again. I figure this is the opportune moment to break the news to him. I got up and went over there to Paul and sat next to him.

"Paul, if I tell you something, will you promise that you will not get upset with me?

He says to me while still smoking his joint, "Just spill it."

As I begin telling him about the situation he's just sitting here looking straight ahead. After I finished talking he pulls the joint out of his mouth, exhaled a cloud of smoke into the air and said, "This was not the deal." He then looks at me. "You said only two weeks!" He gets up out of his chair from under the tree and walks away.

Still sitting here for a minute to collect my thoughts, I then go back over to the porch. My girlfriend asked, "How did it go?"

By not wanting to hurt her feelings I say to her, "It was not as I planned."

She goes on to ask, "Do you have a problem with what has just taken place?"

"No, it's nothing I can't handle," I gave in reply.

Coming out of the house Paul looks at me and begins walking to the main road. We all then get up and goes inside. My girlfriend however, goes into her room gets out a deck of cards calling everyone to the kitchen table to join her. At this point, I am just not up to anything but to get this off of my mind. So we went ahead and start playing a few games. While playing, Paul walks through the door and goes into the bedroom.

My children and my girlfriend looks at me and asks, "What's wrong with your man?"

I said to them, "I can't answer that. And please . . . don't get nothing started."

Paul then comes out of the bedroom invites me to join him in the bathroom, he then starts the shower. While in the shower he asks in a mean tone of voice, "Did you have a talk with your girlfriend?"

To keep from arguing, I say to him, "She says in a few days she is supposed to be going to spend some time with one of her cousins."

After getting out of the shower Paul goes back into the bedroom and I go back into the living room with my girlfriend, and the children not knowing how to face her with this issue, they leave off the go to their bedrooms as well because they know she's making it harder for me I excuse myself and go to bed.

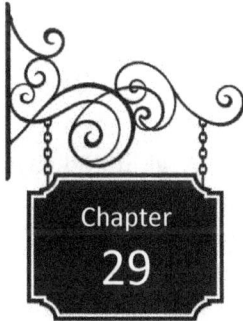

Chapter

29

It is Thanksgiving Eve, also Paul and I's anniversary. Everyone gets up early to begin their day, and Paul having to go work for a few hours. As for me, I have to go and get the rest of the food to make our Thanksgiving dinner. Knowing that I have to go find a ride to the grocery store I go ahead and get dressed and leave the house. Luckily while walking down the street I catch one of the neighbors pulling out of their yard.

After purchasing everything that I needed to begin my dinner, I returned home. While walking through the door, my girlfriend asked, "Is there anything you want me to do?"

Saying to her, "Paul and I are the only ones allowed in the

kitchen."

She and my children then pitched in to do the house cleaning.

Two hours later Paul returns home with a bottle of champagne and a half dozen of roses. Glancing over to notice my girlfriend is giving me this unfamiliar look, I'm trying to figure out what this look is for. So I pretend to be busy. Paul then leaves out of the kitchen and goes into the living room for a few minutes. I stop what I am doing and goes into the bedroom and get Paul's gift. Returning back into the living room I handed it to him, saying, "I wish I could have given you more."

He looks at me and says, "As long as you are still here."

But it puzzles me from the way he says it.

He then says to me, "If you don't mind, I would like to relax for a few minutes."

Going back into the kitchen my girlfriend says to me, "Your man will make me say something I don't want to say, but this is your home." She then gets up from the table and goes into the living room with the children. Paul finally comes out of the room to help with the cooking. As he's getting started, my children gets up and go to their rooms to get prepared for bed. Tired from having such a long day I go get into the shower, hoping that this will be my alone time, . . . lucky me it is not. Paul comes in behind me. He pulls off of his clothes and gets in. We're not saying nothing to each other. By not saying anything, I hurried up and got out.

After getting out of the shower Paul says to me, "Why don't you go ahead into the bedroom while I put the food away. While getting into bed I can hear the conversation between Paul and my girlfriend. He's asking her if she was enjoying herself. And then she let him know that it was okay, but to look at where we are – being that we're in the country. Not being able to hear what else is being said, I went to sleep.

A few minutes later after I had nodded out, here comes

Paul into the bedroom waking me up. Look, I was tired and frustrated, and I didn't really want to hear what anyone had to say, I just wanted to get some sleep. But, for the sake of not getting into an argument, I listened to what he had to say anyway.

Paul said to me, "Hey, I don't like your friend's attitude!"

After giving no response to what he said, Paul decides to leave back out of the room. So, I turned my back and went back to sleep. What a day!

Thanksgiving Day, Paul and I get up early to put the finishing touches on the dinner, we have a few hours before my family gets here. While doing so Paul says to me, "You need to get your children out of bed so they can help out." Upon awakening my children, my girlfriend too then gets out of bed, hating the fact we only have this one bathroom she has a habit of spending a lot of time in there only to get Paul upset with my children.

I hurried down the hallway saying to my children, "Don't do anything, just go straight into the bathroom." My son then rushed out of his room and went in. One hour later my children and my girlfriend got dressed and came into the living room. Seconds later Paul's nephew pulls into the driveway, Paul then goes outside. Immediately after, my brother and his wife arrives and Paul and his nephew leaves out of the yard.

After getting inside my sister-in-law asked, "Do you guys have a can of cranberry sauce for the dinner?" Telling her that I had forgotten all about it, she informs me that the reason for asking was because Paul wanted me to go to the store to buy a can for dinner. She then leaves out of the house to go to the store. While setting the table the rest of the family arrives, including Paul and his nephew with all the preparation of the foods; the rest of the family arrives as well. Haven't had the chance to change my clothes, I figured that I better start getting myself ready.

Paul, being one who just came in too, asked, "Have you gotten me anything out to wear? And if not, can you get me some clothing? . . . And make sure they are ironed." Looking at him and saying to myself that he could have did this earlier before he left the house, but instead waited until company comes to want to do this now.

Upon getting into the bedroom to take a break, I sit down on the bed to relax a little. I guess by taking so long Paul decides to come into the room to check on me. "Babe, you need to hurry up because everyone is waiting on you." My mouth dropped – oh, I wanted to say something so bad. After I finally got situated, minutes later I went into the kitchen to join everyone else.

While serving the food, Paul looks at my sister-in-law and asked, "Did you go get the cranberry sauce?"

She said to him that she too had forgotten it, but within a mean tone of voice. He looks over at her and says, "How do you forget cranberry sauce which makes the dinner?"

Knowing where this is going I begin telling jokes around the table about the sauce to calm things down, but unfortunately that didn't happen. My brother gets up out of his seat and says to Paul, "Listen man, my wife said she forgot, . . . so you need to get off her with it before you get me upset."

Everyone asking the both of them to calm down.

My brother's wife then takes him outside to cool things down, while we all talk with Paul. He *meaning Paul* finally calms down. So I called my brother and his wife back inside, and then we all said grace and served dinner.

My son sitting next to me said quietly, "Mom, did you see how your man tried to upset our dinner?"

Replying in a low tone, "It's okay, let's just enjoy this moment."

After dinner, we were all having such a great time. We began playing different types of games and taking family memorial pictures for keepsake.

Hours has gone pass and everyone is beginning to leave. Paul feeling a little tired said, "I need to take a nap." He then goes into the bedroom.

After seeing everyone off I then begin to put everything away and start cleaning up the place. While working on the kitchen, my girlfriend walks up to me and says, "I noticed your man love to nitpick with people. All of what he did earlier was not called for. And over a can of cranberry sauce, . . . really?"

Not missing a beat in my cleaning, I said, "Now you see what I have to go through."

She placed her hand on my shoulder for a second to give me pause for a moment from cleaning and said, "You're a good woman, don't let anyone tell you different."

Leaving me alone to continue attending to my cleaning, my girlfriend then turns away and goes into her bedroom. Being that I am now alone, I – myself is becoming sleepy.

I guess I'm gonna have to leave some of my work undone because I'm tired. So I went into my bedroom and laid across the bed. And sure as a cactus plant without water, Paul turns over towards me and decides to put his arms around me asking, "Did you have a good time?"

Being tired, I mumbled that I enjoyed my family. He then looked at me; his body shadowing my back for a moment, and then he removes his arm and distance himself. For me, one way or another . . . I didn't care, so I called it a night.

Chapter
30

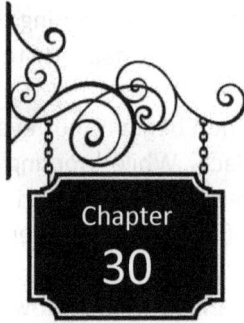

Three months later, my girlfriend is still here and things are getting out of control. Being that she is now going through changes, it seems she's taking it out on everyone who is around. Not wanting to leave her here alone because I have to go to work and my children are going to school, I said to her, "Try to make yourself comfortable, and after I return home we will find something to do that will pick you up."

Hours later I return home to find my girlfriend have already made dinner. I said to myself, "Now why did she go and do this, when I had already told her that Paul does not allow no one else to cook in our kitchen? And if he finds out she made the dinner, he's going to be very upset and will not eat." But, I know that what's done is done. I just will have to play it off as if it's okay.

So I go into the bedroom and put my things away – thinking what am I going to tell Paul if he ask 'did I cooked this,' and knowing he knows how I cook. As my children comes through the door, they can smell something cooking in the kitchen. They put their school things down and went to see what it was. When they looked at what's cooking, they said, "Mom, tell us you didn't cooked this food?"

"No, I didn't. But please don't say a word about it to

Paul."

Upon already sitting at the table contemplating what to do, my girlfriend goes ahead and calls everyone to the table. My children came back in and sat at the table looking at their plates, then at each other. Refusing to eat the food that's before them, they excused themselves. But before they left the table, they both said to her, "We're not hungry . . . we ate enough at school. But thank you though."

Trying not to make her feel bad I fixed me a plate and returned back to my seat at the table. As I started tasting it, my palate told me that was enough – that it was time to put the fork down and drink some water. I really didn't know what to think, except that I cannot eat it.

As she continued to eat her own cooking, she paused for a moment, then looked over at me and asked, "What does it taste like?"

I smiled, trying to swallow my water. "Yep (giving her the thumbs up), it's okay."

She smiled and finished cleaning off her plate, while I patiently waited until she was done. Finally, she's all done and going into the living room. As she walks out I quickly lift my plate off the table, scoot the food to the edge of the plate, and dumped it in the trash.

As the time get closer for Paul to return home I say to my girlfriend, "What you cooked was good, but it isn't what I had in mind." I then go into the kitchen and starts something different – so whenever Paul gets here, I won't have to argue.

6:00pm Paul is home. After getting in he goes into the kitchen and looks in the pots, then walks away and goes into the bedroom. A second later I am being called into the room. As I walks into the room I am being questioned.

"Who cooked that food?"

Hearing my girlfriend walking down the hallway, I was kinda hoping she would be going into her room. Instead, she stands at the door of our bedroom and says, "Paul, I was only trying to help out, . . . so I made the dinner." And then she walks away.

Paul then says to me, "I want you to tell her – do not cook anymore in this house!"

Not wanting to blow this out of the water, I just said, "I'll make sure she gets the message."

Going back into the kitchen I fixed my children something to eat that I had made. My girlfriend seeing this, gets up and goes outside and sits on the front porch.

I said to my children, "You guys really hurt her feelings. You should have at least eaten a little something that she cooked."

They both look at me and said, "Are you crazy?!"

Feeling bad myself, I go outside to apologize – saying to her, "I am so sorry how things turned out. I know you wanted help, and no one means any harm. We just don't eat what you eat."

Paul comes out of the room acting all ignorant.

"I'm hungry! . . . And I am not about to eat what she cooked!"

I said to him, "I have already made you something different."

He fixes himself something to eat and goes into the living room with it, then sits down to get his grub on. My girlfriend then comes back inside and approaches him. "Hey, Paul. Did you taste any of my food?"

He lies and says, "Yes."

She then sits down near him and begin telling him of all the seasonings that she added into her pots; right after Paul had told that lie. I just can't believe it! I am sitting here with an amazed look on my face, saying to myself, "If she cooks again I am going to make you eat it."

Thinking that what was said earlier is behind us now.

It's gotten late, and Paul then gets up and says to me, "I am going to take a shower and I would like for you to join me."

Thinking that he might be feeling a little frisky, I decide go into the bathroom right behind him.

But to my surprise, this negro had something else in mind.

Paul turning around with an evil look on his face and over-towering me says, "I am not playing with you! And I am not going to say it again! . . . Do not allow her over my stove!"

Damn! Ain't that a bitch!

Now that I am so effen' tired of him repeating this to me, I say to him, "If it's bothering you that much, why don't you tell her yourself?!"

I then walk out of the bathroom.

You can hear him yelling for me to come back. I'm not that stupid. I continued into the bedroom and sat on the bed. After he finishes and gets out, I then double-back and take me a shower. Afterwards, I get into bed and call it a night.

Chapter
31

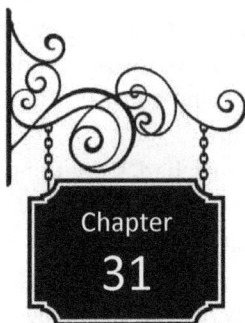

Weeks and months have now gone by, and now things are worse than before. My girlfriend has really made matters worse between me, my children, and Paul. Having a busy day, we are all up early – my children going to school and Paul and I going to work; which I don't have that many hours to work.

Sitting here at my job, I am trying to figure out what is my girlfriend up to and the reason for it all. But I have to make the best of my day.

It is 11:00am, my time is now up and I am on my way home. I get home to find the usual, my girlfriend is still sitting around in her night clothing watching television.

By seeing her this way, I asked, "Are you feeling okay?"

She says to me, "I feel fine. I just didn't feel like changing out of my night clothing because I haven't brought much clothing with me. And besides, I have no way to the laundry room."

Not wanting to say nothing foul to her, I walked away.

While doing what needs to be done before Paul and my children returns home, she says to me, "Hopefully, I will be going back upstate soon."

Saying to myself, "Thank you," and I continued on.

3:00pm. My children returns home from school. As the two them settled down I go ahead and fix them a snack until dinner is ready. While sitting at the table my daughter's passing me a piece of paper from school, which states within a few days her class will be going on a field trip to Washington DC. Being it is a last minute notice, I have to come up with a certain amount of money.

Volunteering, my girlfriend says to my daughter, "I will be doing your hair for the trip, and I will start after you finishes your chores."

Meanwhile, my children begin their chores and I'll get dinner started. But for whatever reason, everyone wants something baked today. I'm thinking it might will be quick and easy. So I go along with them. An hour later, my children are done with their chores and my girlfriend then starts on my daughter's hair. While doing her hair, my girlfriend decides to put a little fun in it.

Time escaping away into the evening, the day has been nice so far. We're sitting around laughing and talking, then all of a sudden Paul walks through the door and into the living room, and sits down. I decide to go sit with him for a few minutes.

While talking to him and thinking . . . I smell something burning, "Daughter, can you take a few seconds and turn the oven off?"

Not wanting her to move, my girlfriend says to me, "Give me a minute, and I'll check it and turn it off."

Give me a minute? . . . I got up and told her, "Never mind, I'll do it!"

Getting up to do so, Paul goes into a rage, yelling and screaming – saying to me, "Come back here and sit your ass down!!!" He continues, "Didn't you just tell your daughter to do it?!"

Saying to him, "I can do it myself!"

He is constantly going on and on, he then calls me stupid, asking, "Which one of you is the mother here?"

I said bluntly, "I am her mother!"

He just continued cursing at me. He says to me, "No, you're not. You're the other mother."

Knowing what he means, I say to him, "I never suckered you out of anything."

He begins calling me every curse word that he can think of – all except my name.

I am trying so hard to ignore him, but on and on he goes.

Now he's being flat out disrespectful. He says, "Your daddy was a punk!"

He has hit a bad nerve with my girlfriend also, and we both lost all control with our mouths, saying to this jackass, "I am not going to allow you to talk about my father when he's no longer here on this earth." Before even thinking, I say to him, "if anybody's daddy is a punk, it was yours! . . . Especially from the stories I've been told. And besides, my father stayed with my mother and raised all of his children . . . unlike your daddy – who just walked out and left you guys."

My girlfriend jumping up from the table saying to Paul also, "I will not sit here and have you talk about her father the way you are."

Paul then turns his attention towards my girlfriend and said to her, "If you don't like it, you can leave!"

She goes on to say, "Gladly!" Back and forth cursing at each other.

As my girlfriend and I walk toward the backdoor to go outside, Paul picks up his beer and throws it at me – but not hitting me. I then turn around and to go back into the living room. My children not liking what they saw knew that there was great hostility in the air and just wanted me to be safe. They then began pushing me to the backdoor a little faster to prevent me from doing something that we might regret.

My girlfriend, my children, and I went and sat on the steps.

She says to my son, "If I were you, I would have jumped

him when I got the chance!"

I looked at her and said, "I will not allow my children to fight my battles."

Getting upset after my girlfriend said what she did to my son, I got up and went back inside. As I was walking pass Paul, he is all of a sudden pretending to be asleep. I didn't buy this for a second.

Minutes later, my girlfriend and my children comes inside and goes to their rooms. Getting tired of looking at Paul with his pretending self, I walked away and went into my bedroom grabbed my night things and the radio, and headed into the bathroom to take a shower and listen to some music to calm myself down. I then turned the water on and jumped in.

As one of my favorite song begins to play on the radio I begin to sing. While singing to it, I hear my girlfriend laughing loudly. I Thought that she was talking with my children until I realized the lyrics of the song, which had caught her attention.

After showering I go back into the living room to make sure the doors are secure. Hearing me walking around, Paul jumps up off of the couch and goes into the bedroom, he gets his things and goes into the bathroom and takes a shower as well. When my girlfriend detected that it was all clear, she comes out of her bedroom and says to me, "I just had to laugh when that song came on. I guess his love don't live here anymore."

Saying to her in a humorous and serious way, "It is slowly going out of the window."

My children too returned into the living room when they knew that me and my girlfriend was in there. We all picked some games out and played and talked until we can longer stay awake.

We then said our goodnights.

The following morning I am being awaken with a kiss on the forehead by Paul. He's acting as if nothing happened last night.

Leaning down by my side of the bed he says to me, "I am

sorry about last night, but I want you to see that your girlfriend is trying to take over our home. For one thing, having your children not do what you tell them to do." He goes on to say, "You need to watch out for her."

Looking him in the face and saying to him, "I will not allow that to happen . . . and how can you just show out the way you did in front of my company? And you know what? . . . You took it a little too far this time." Then, I got to thinking on what he just said. "Hum . . . yeah, . . . I've noticed the changes in her attitude toward me." I figured that there were some sense in what he just mentioned, but it still doesn't excuse the violent behavior, if he truly loves me.

He then gets up and gets himself ready for work.

Upon awakening my children, I received a phone call from my nephew saying he's coming to stay the weekend with me and my children. Giving him the okay, we cut our conversation short and hung up the phone.

Seconds later, the phone rings again, this time it's the lady from down the street asking if I can help her out later this afternoon. It was a matter of needing some money – I agree to do so.

Chapter
32

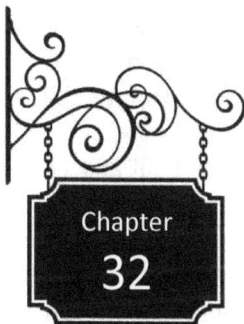

While waiting on my nephew to arrive my children and I decided to go visit my mother for a little while so that they can spend some time with some of their friends, and I too can visit some of mine.

It is now 4:00pm, time to return home so I can go to work. Shortly after getting home my nephew arrives. As we go inside Paul pulls into the driveway, he says to me, "I am getting off from work early because I am tired."

I then I told him that I have to go help the lady out down the street, and before leaving he needs to take his key with him, because my girlfriend may go with me. Before walking out the door, Paul said that he figured we should be returning home around the same time, then he left.

After getting inside I invited my girlfriend to go with us. She says to me, "Hun, I'm just a little tired right now, and I'm probably going to just take me a bath and wait until someone comes over to pick me up."

My children and I were okay with it, then we left the house.

Within thirty minutes I am finished with what was needed. So we left to go home – to make the walk shorter, the children began making wise jokes about my girlfriend and Paul.

In minutes, we were home walking into the yard. Paul and his nephew are sitting in the car when we arrived.

Paul says to me, "Send the children on the inside because I have something to tell you."

I then send the children inside. Paul and nephew then explained the situation. "When we returned to the house the door was locked, and I thought you was on the inside. So I knocked on the door and your girlfriend came to the door with a towel half-wrapped around her." While his nephew was nodding in agreement, Paul continued, "I then ask her if you were home. When she said no, I told her that I will come inside when you get here."

After telling me what happened, I went inside and approached her asking, "What had taken place while I was away?"

She tried to explain it to me. But I just kept looking at her as she goes on trying . . . "And, . . ."

"And I thought it was you knocking on the door. So I jumped out of the shower grabbed my towel and ran to the door, but I did not know it was Paul and his nephew."

Paul then comes inside and goes into the bedroom. Going in behind him he says to me, "Now you see what's going on?"

I said to him, "I don't like it at all, but I better not never come home and catch the two of you together, . . . because you will not disrespect our home. And besides, this should teach you to sometimes watch what you're saying because you sometimes let dirty words comes out of your mouth, and you gave her the impression that maybe you wanted her in some type of way."

Stunned by what I said, he immediately jumps up off the bed and tells me that he is going to make dinner.

Now here's a twist – I'm overhearing my son saying to his cousin *my nephew*, "I really believe Paul wants to tap that!"

Hearing them still talking about it, I quickly ran over to

my son's room banging on the door, telling them to leave that subject alone.

"Okay, Mom."

"Yes, Auntie."

"That's better! Now get yourselves ready, we'll be having dinner in a moment."

Seems like within less than 15 minutes, Paul's calling everyone to the dinner table. The children and I went in the kitchen to eat. He then goes and takes a shower. Not crossing paths, my girlfriend comes out of her room and goes into the living room and sat down. After awhile, she's just sitting there. I am thinking maybe she's ashamed. I excuse myself from the table and goes to sit by her.

I asked, "Can you please tell me what is going on with you?"

She's not saying a word. Not wanting to push the issue I left her alone.

As my children leaves the table and go into their bedrooms, she asks, "Where is Paul?"

Saying to her, "In the shower."

Then she goes on to ask something odd. "Do you and Paul ever have sex?"

Amazed that she asked me a personal question like this, in response I asked, "Why are you asking me this?"

"Because I never hear anything going on in your bedroom."

My eyes pop's wide open – asking her, "Are you listening to what's going on in my bedroom?!"

She says to me, "No, it's just strange to me."

Becoming upset from the question, I decided to go to bed.

Upon getting into my bedroom I sat on the bed next to Paul asking him, "Have you been talking with my girlfriend about our bedroom business?"

His reply other than just saying a simple 'no' was, "Why are you asking?"

Wow! A reply I wish not to give, but I have to. "Because she asked me *do we have sex*."

He gets upset and says, "If she wants to hear something, . . . I am going to give her something to hear." He then says to me, "Go ahead and take you a shower."

Without questioning at the time, I go and jump into the shower.

Now I am really thinking. Just maybe, he has been talking with her – only because we haven't been having sex. And the reason being is, because either he's high or he comes home and starts an argument . . . so we won't.

After getting out of the shower I go into the living room and sit for a second with my girlfriend; just to get that sense of feeling that something is off. We gave our little smiley chitchat among each other, and then we say our goodnights.

As I go back into the bedroom Paul says to me, "Sit down on the bed."

I am looking at him thinking to myself *what are you about to start,* asking the question, "Why?"

He says to me, "I am going to give her something to think about."

He then begins bouncing up and down on the bed and requests that I do the same. We then begin making all kinds of noises.

I said, "Paul, we have children in the house."

He then says, "Never mind them!"

Thinking to myself, "This will not look good for us."

We continued bouncing on the bed . . . suddenly, I hear my girlfriend going into her room, but never hearing the door being closed.

Paul says to me, "Doing all of this has now gotten me excited!"

We're looking at each other smiling. "So am I! . . . First, let me go and check on my children, and then I'll be right back."

I get up and go into my daughter's room (who is now awake) explains to her from what she heard was only a joke that we played on my girlfriend. I then go into my son's room (awake also) explains the same to him and my nephew – they're just sitting there with a crazy look on their faces. But when I went further down into the hallway, I noticed that my girlfriend's room door is still open. I stopped by her room, but it seems like she was expecting me.

She asks, "Do you feel better?"

I replied, "What do you mean?"

She looks at me and smiles while watching me as I am walking out of her room.

I said to myself, "If only you knew."

Upon getting back into my bedroom, Paul looking at me asking, "Are you tired?"

Saying yes, he then says to me, "I am ready I get off of the bed and sit on the loveseat," that's at the foot of our bed.

Paul comes over and begins kissing me on my neck, but the thought no one is asleep, he then says to me, "We are already on the chair."

But not wanting to upset him, I go ahead with what we started – not what I was expecting. So we then called it a night.

Chapter
33

A few days later, things are about the same and it's getting worse with my girlfriend. She's beginning to pick fights with my children.

Having to go shopping and run a few errands I ask my girlfriend to assist my children while they do their chores until they're done. She agreed. "Yes, of course. I will make sure they are done." I then leave the house and begin my day.

Being out for a few hours and getting everything done, I returned home. Upon walking into the house, I noticed that my girlfriend is very upset. Not asking any questions, I go ahead and put the things away.

Minutes later, she says to me, "Your children would not listen to nothing I told them to do."

I called the two of them out of their rooms into the kitchen. "What is wrong with you guys?!"

They both say to me, "She need to tell the truth! She's been cursing at us the minute you walked out of the door – until you almost returned."

Turning to her, I said, "I do not like the fact that you are cursing at my children, . . . because I do not curse them."

She then responded sarcastically, "Well, I don't want nothing else to do with them!"

Returning the favor *so-to-speak*, "Thank you!" I continued on with what I began.

It's 6:00pm. Paul returns home from work. As he walks into the house he says to me, "I have to leave to go on another job. And if it is not a problem, will I be able to assist him in doing so?"

Gladly he had asked, and I say yes.

Upon grabbing my purse and on the way out of the door, I told my children to stay in their rooms until we return. As we were leaving the house, I decided to bring up the conversation about my girlfriend, but all Paul is saying to me is that I invited the cockroach in.

"Now either you tell her or I will. Either which way, she's got to get out!"

Paul appeared very serious, so I said, "Let me do it because knowing you, you will make this ugly."

He just looked at me and smirked.

I ignored it and continued. "And it will cause a huge problem between our friendship."

He shook his head like *whatever* while we walked to his company truck.

"Paul, . . . her and I have been friends for too many years to let all that happen."

While performing the job there's nothing but silence between the two of us. I started asking myself, "Why is this happening to me?"

After completing the job we returned home. The children are on the outside playing as Paul goes inside of the house I went over to my children asking them, "Were there any problems since I left here?"

They both said to me that they were okay.

I then go on the inside to relax a while. My girlfriend then walks up to me and asked, "So what did your man have to say to you, for the simple reason why he took you with him?"

I said to her in a nice way, "He wanted to know when are you leaving to go home."

She looks at me and says, "Soon!" She then places one hand on her hip while waving the other in a circular motion and said, "I am asking you, . . . girlfriend . . . are you tired of me?"

Wanting to say yes, but I know it will hurt her feelings – and I don't want to lie to her neither. I had to tell her no, even though it may cause more problems; she's my friend.

My girlfriend back to smiling again, gave me a hug and walks away; heading back into her bedroom. As I go into the kitchen to prepare the dinner I noticed the gas is beginning to get low – thinking what else can go wrong, because it is getting cold outside and we cook and warm up our home with gas.

Upon going into the bedroom to sit on the bed next to Paul, I try to slowly break it to him of our gas situation. He says to me, "Well, we'll only use the gas to cook with, and you will use the kerosene to warm up with."

By looking at him, I'm wanting to say I don't like it, and I can't handle it, nor can anyone else. But I have no other choice.

I went to talk to my girlfriend and tried to explain it to her about the situation, she says to me, "You cannot do that because it causes my asthma to flare up, and the smell will be in all of our clothing."

Understanding what she's saying, but I cannot argue about it.

Minutes later, Paul leaves the house to go obtain the oil for the heaters. In order to save gas I hurried up and made a quick dinner, hoping that the heat lasts a long enough time to keep the house a little warmer until we get prepared for the following day.

While sitting at the dinner table Paul walks through the door. He goes down the hallway to fill the heater. My girlfriend – on the other hand, says to me, "I guess this is the way, huh? . . . As to run me away."

Seconds later, Paul calls me into our bedroom wondering what is this all about. He says to me just as my girlfriend had mentioned, saying that this should get rid of her.

Looking at him and saying to myself, "You are so wrong."

I don't even bother to go back and have dinner, instead I go ahead and get into the shower. Simply because at this point I am being torn between the two of them.

After showering, I then go and lay across my bed. Upon falling asleep, I am being awakened by Paul shaking me and saying that I need to go check on my friend, because he thinks that she has hurt herself.

Immediately jumping out of bed, I run into her room only to find out that she's lying on the floor asking me what had happened.

She says to me, "I don't know how it happened, but my bed fell apart."

Helping her up from the floor and making sure she's okay, she says to me, "I know he wants me out, and I know he is also trying to make me uncomfortable."

Trying not to cause anymore confusing, I try to sugarcoat it with her saying that he is just going through one of his little moments. After making it comfortable for her to sleep, I returned to my bedroom and calls it a night.

Chapter
34

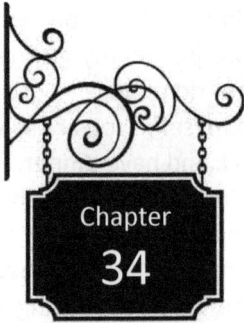

The next day Paul getting up early to get ready for work thinking that I am asleep, he leaves out of the bedroom. Lying here till after hearing the backdoor closes, I get out of bed and go into the hallway and noticed that the house is very cold.

Thinking that the oil must have burned out, I then go to check the heaters. Well, I think not. To my surprise Paul turned all of them off. Seconds later the telephone rings. This is no coincidence, it's Paul. And he's asking is everyone still in bed.

After saying yes, he then says to me, "I turned the heaters off since it seems like no one was trying to get up."

I wanted to climb through the phone so bad, . . . but I can't say a word, so I just hung up.

Going into everyone's rooms I tell them to stay warm. "You guys need to put on more clothes."

My girlfriend says to me, "I really wasn't planning to get up because this house is really too cold for me to move."

As I go back into my bedroom to get dressed for the day, there's a knock at the backdoor. It's the landlord. I invited her to come inside. She says to me, "I am going to make this short because it is too cold in here, but I want you all to know that I am going up on the rent, and it's because your girlfriend is here. And by she's getting a check, I have to go up $100.00 more and I am not changing my mind."

I looked around the house, then looked at my landlord and said, "So you are going up on the rent cause of my girlfriend's visiting?" Boy, was I pissed.

She then gets up and leaves out of the house, still talking to herself as she gets into her car.

Thinking how could this happen and why are we having to pay $400.00 living out here in these woods. Also, my hours have gotten cut on my job and Paul money is coming up short.

My girlfriend comes out of her room saying, "I heard the conversation between you and the landlord. So how is your landlord charging you for having a guest in your home?"

I replied, "We will discuss this when Paul comes home."

Being that it was too cold to do anything about it, we all just sat down and laid around the house. With the gas almost out and just watching television, I make sandwiches and snacks for everyone. Time has passed, Paul comes home from work.

After sending my children to their rooms, I invite Paul and my girlfriend to join me at the kitchen table. Speaking to him on the issue with the landlord, he says, "Call her and tell her that we are not paying that kind of money!"

My girlfriend looks at the two of us and says, "I cannot spare $100.00 a month out of my check."

Paul almost going through the roof, his mouth is about to move the wrong way – if you know what I mean, but before doing so, I get up from the table and go into the living room and calls the landlord.

I let her know that Paul says we prefer to move.

She says to me, "Well then, you all can just get out of my house."

I responded with, "We will be out in the next thirty days."

She went a step further, she replied, "No, I want you all out in fifteen days!"

After I heard that, I then hung up the phone.

Not knowing where we are going to go in such a short notice, Paul says to me, "I will go and have a talk with my uncle so that the two of us can stay with him for a few days. But your children have to go stay with your mother."

I said to him, "My children will not be going to my mother's."

He looked at me and walked away.

Returning back into the living room my girlfriend says to me, "Don't you think it will best if you leave him and the two of us can get a place together?"

When she said this, my mouth completely dropped. She looked at me as expecting me to say something. I am hoping she doesn't think that I'm agreeing on this, but I guess she has more to say.

So she continued, "Look hun, . . . it's because your children don't need this. What they need . . . is to be settled."

Whoa! I really didn't need to hear all this – *at a time like this*.

I told her, "No, . . . you look! I am not trying to hurt your feelings, but you and I cannot stay in the same house!"

She then gets upset and goes into her room.

Feeling bad from everything that is happening, I go and get into the shower. Paul comes in afterwards asking if he can join me. But before I can say a word, he's already pulling off his clothes and getting in.

He's back to hanging on this attitude without saying nothing to me, which at this point I can care less.

After getting out of the shower we both go into the bedroom. He's sitting here with an angry look on his face.

All of a sudden he asks me, "What kind of friend do you have?" Before answering, he goes on to say, "When the boat begins to sink, the rats will jump off!" Still trying to make me feel bad, he adlibs by saying, "You invited her here!"

That's just great! He just keeps going on and on, and on.

I thought going into the bedroom would give Paul time enough to calm down – no matter what happens, he's always putting the fault on me. I am so tired of having to suck things up and living my life like this.

It really makes me feel like me and my children are being used as if we are his personal dartboard; a target to throw his fiery darts at.

But one of these days he will know.

Being that it has gotten late and it is so cold in here, I go and get into bed. Shortly after, Paul follows behind me and gets in too. As him and his attitude rolls over to snuggle, so am I with my back towards him and pretending to be asleep.

I call it a night, because tomorrow is going to be another day of hell.